INVINCIBLE SPIRITS

INVINCIBLE SPIRITS

A Thousand Years
of Women's Spiritual Writings

Compiled by

Felicity Leng

WILLIAM B. EERDMANS PUBLISHING COMPANY
GRAND RAPIDS, MICHIGAN / CAMBRIDGE, U.K.

First published 2006 in the United Kingdom by
the Canterbury Press Norwich
9–17 St Albans Place, London
N1 0NX

This edition published 2007
in the United States of America by
Wm. B. Eerdmans Publishing Co.
2140 Oak Industrial Drive N.E., Grand Rapids, Michigan 49505 /
P.O. Box 163, Cambridge CB3 9PU U.K.

Printed in the United States of America

12 11 10 09 08 07   7 6 5 4 3 2 1

ISBN 978-0-8028-2453-0

www.eerdmans.com

Contents

Contents

Preface

The original inspiration for this book dates from the time, some years ago, when I lived in Uzès, still an essentially medieval town in the south of France. Dhuoda, a Christian noblewoman, was exiled there in the ninth century and wrote a poignant self-help book for her estranged adolescent son, William. When I read the book, I was not only interested in the ascertainable details of her life and her learning, but moved by her predicament, her introspective method and her skill in advising the son whom she never saw again. I decided to find out all I could about Dhuoda and to write about her life. Eventually, when discussing the project, Christine Smith of Canterbury Press suggested that I should produce an anthology of women spiritual writers rather than concentrate on one author. The result is this book.

Evelyn Underhill reminds us that 'every religion looks for, and most have possessed, some revealer of the Spirit' (*The Life of the Spirit and the Life of To-day*). It has been a privilege to have read works by so many brilliant women who have revealed such varied aspects of the Spirit, often in the most demanding circumstances, and not only from the viewpoints of the main Christian churches but from those of many different nonconforming traditions. Admittedly, a lifetime of study and dedication would be needed to read and do justice to the works of even the few women spiritual writers selected for this anthology. Therefore I have not tried to produce anything like a comprehensive array of women spiritual writers but have chosen authors whose work can still appeal beneficially to twenty-first-century readers seeking spiritual guidance and direction. I have tried to emphasize works which, if explored proficiently, could become sources of ideas and creative insights for self-development, lead to a deeper understanding of Christianity, and help us in today's frenetic world. Unfortunately, we are increasingly invited to exist in virtually real terms rather than experience genuine affective and intellectual relations with our fellow humans. Reading the letters of certain writers of the past makes us aware of what we have lost or are in the process of losing, especially when they show real concern and affection for the recipients, when relationships are built slowly and deliberately, and when writers have taken time to think about their correspondents' problems, and give them advice and wisdom tailored to their predicaments.

The anthology is divided into sections corresponding to the main elements of most spiritual quests. The first is devoted to love, the kernel of the Christian message and the essential inspiration if not the immediate topic of most of these women's, especially the mystics', writings. It continues in some way throughout the remaining sections, for instance in that devoted to creativity and visions: that is, to love as creation. To create, of course, is a Trinitarian and fundamentally Christian function (cf. Dorothy L. Sayers, *The Mind of The Maker*). We are created to create. By nature and often by circumstances, we are called to discover and express our 'thisness'; to find our true selves; to be uniquely creative human beings, and to express the love that has been created to exist in and through us.

The theme persists even in sections that might seem initially to be far removed from ecstatic communion with God. These contain pieces that describe not – or not merely – sublime visions but the moments of weakness, doubt and disbelief that are painful yet inescapable accompaniments of convictions courageously maintained and defended for the sake of truth to love.

I have also tried to convey something of the 'divine fecundity' that passes down the generations. Almost all the women represented here would seem to have had their spiritual children, who then modified the message and transmitted their particular inspiration to future generations for rehandling in the light of new spiritual experience. Powerful women writers and saints reappear in the form of reworked insights or resounding echoes in later centuries. St Cecilia so impressed Julian of Norwich that reflection on her predecessor's legend led Julian to write on the 'three wounds'. Madame Guyon was wholly captivated by the life of St Jeanne de Chantal and ventured on the impossible task of imitating everything her model had done. St Teresa of Avila's mystical experiences not only inspired the rich and extraordinarily various contemplative life of the Carmelite order but affected many women outside the religious life. Emily Brontë's work influenced Emily Dickinson's metaphysical verse and Margiad Evans' self-understanding. Evans had intended to write a book on Emily Brontë's progress from nature mysticism through religious mysticism to what she termed 'universal and ultimate mysticism', but might be said instead to have taken this road in her own works.

My training as an artist has made me interested in the sources of inspiration of the writers I have chosen, and the connections between them. As work progressed on this anthology, I found that passages from the Old and New Testaments resonated through most of the women's writings, from Hroswitha and Dhuoda to such disparate sensibilities as those of St Thérèse of Lisieux, Mary Baker Eddy and Margiad Evans. Perhaps Hildegard of Bingen's advice to 'drench your thoughts in the streams of scripture and study the example of the saints, then try to live like them' encapsulates the traditional spiritual education for beginners on the spiritual path. The work of the passionate and erudite Ida Görres seems to obey Hildegard's recommendation perfectly. She writes with verve and authority on numerous subjects and people, including Julian of Norwich, Florence Nightingale, the Revelations of St Bridget, von Hügel's study of St Catherine of Genoa, Mary Ward, and Thérèse of Lisieux, welding them all into her own thought, and continually returning to Psalm 118 for solace.

Of course no writer's work comes out of a vacuum. Although many purely literary writers' work is best appreciated without reference to their sometimes tedious and irrelevant histories, this is not the case with essentially spiritual artists. What we can learn of each of these women's lives should be studied in conjunction with their work to gain a full appreciation of the whole person and the creative working of the Divine through them. It is

reassuring to learn that many of these exceptional women over-
came, and turned to significant ends, such difficult circumstances
as the early loss of a parent or parents, poverty, chronic illness,
being of the wrong gender in a male-dominated environment or
profession, or a lack of recognition by their contemporaries. They
transformed the original dross into gold in the magical laboratory
of the spirit, and the strange alchemy even of trials and torment,
and emerged with renewed energy to develop as extraordinary
beings and signs of love and understanding for all humankind.

The lives of many of the writers whom I have included in this
selection seem to follow a certain pattern. There is an early reali-
zation of their singularity and a sense of being called by God,
then a period of inner conflict and withdrawal or falling prey to
some illness, after which they re-create themselves and emerge
as more defined, or connected, persons, or achieve an inner
power that drives them to communicate or lead and guide in a
world-changing way. St Catherine of Genoa spent four years in
turmoil and disillusionment before becoming a hospital matron
and teacher. St Teresa of Avila's lengthy and tortuous struggles
led her to become a founder and reformer. St Catherine of Siena
spent three years living alone before embarking on her active life.
Florence Nightingale felt called by God at seventeen but was in
her thirties before she was able to embark on her remarkable
career.

I hope that readers will be encouraged by these women and
helped to see that by following such examples (but as their own
capabilities decide) they too can arouse the self-satisfied to risk
and creativity, bring healing into tired and fractured lives, and
help others to advance through mystery towards the numinous.

Felicity Leng

Lisieux, France
2006

Love and Fulfilment

꿏

ANGELA OF FOLIGNO

Angela of Foligno describes the process by which lover and divine Beloved are joined in a mystic union.

An iron in the fire

When you put a hot iron in the fire it assumes the very shape and nature of the fire itself: heat, colour, strength and influence. In fact, it almost turns into the actual fire itself, for it surrenders itself whole and entire and not in part, yet it keeps its own substance. Just so, when the perfect fire of divine love joins the soul to God and unites it with him, it bestows itself on him so to speak totally, and casts itself into God. When it is changed into God, yet without losing its own substance, its whole existence is altered. Then this love makes it almost entirely divine. But knowledge is necessary before this change can take place; then, after knowledge, comes love, and then the lover is transformed into the Beloved.

Liber visionum (Book of Divine Consolation), Book XXXIV, Alcalá, 1502

ST CATHERINE OF GENOA

Catherine of Genoa describes the almost physical pain resulting from the irresistible demands of true love. Its symptoms are similar to those of solitary confinement, and even of certain psychiatrically classifiable conditions.

I

Greater fire

Pure love loves God without why or wherefore. Since love took over the care of everything, I have not taken care of anything, nor have I been able to work with my intellect, memory and will, any more than if I had never had them. Indeed every day I feel myself more occupied in him, and with greater fire. I had given the keys of the house to love, with ample permission to do all that was necessary, and determined to have no consideration for soul or body, but to see that, of all that the law of pure love required, there should not be wanting the slightest particle. And I stood so occupied in contemplating this work of love, that if he had cast me, body and soul, into hell, hell itself would have appeared to me all love and consolation. . . .

Yet the corresponding, increasing constraint of the false self is most real. I find myself every day more restricted, as if someone were (first) confined within the walls of a city, then in a house with an ample garden, then in a house without a garden, then in a hall, then in a room, then in an ante-room, then in the cellar of the house with but little light, then in a prison without any light at all; and then her hands were tied and her feet were in the stocks, and then her eyes were bandaged, and then she would not be given anything to eat, and then no one would be able to speak to her; and then, to crown all, every hope were taken from her of leaving there as long as life lasted. Nor would any other comfort remain to such a person, than the knowledge that it was God who was doing all this, through love with great mercy; an insight which would give her great contentment. And yet this contentment does not diminish the pain or the oppression.

Friedrich von Hügel, *The Mystical Element of Religion as Studied in Saint Catherine of Genoa and Her Friends*, Vol. I, London, 1908, pp. 268–9

JEANNE-MARIE BOUVIER DE LA MOTTE-GUYON

Madame Guyon saw her mission as the 'destruction of reason alone' and the 'contradiction of men' as a practical necessity to accomplish this end. She wrote a number of popular works on subjects such as 'spiritual torrents' and the stages by which the mind could be subjugated in order to liberate the divine energy within the individual.

The ocean of divine love

Shadowy ray cast by a great light;
Night, yet luminous flood:
Pure love, plain and simple truth,
Source of all goodness, and first cause!

Tender centre of peace and rest, heavenly delight,
Holy moment of glory,
Gentle knot of pure unity,
Absorption of all sweet remembrance.

Noble majesty, utter and unchanging love,
Pure essence of loving kindness,
Night brighter than day,
Your light hastens towards infinity.

But this illumination is dark for me.
It is an impenetrable abyss,
Even though my heart knows
It is the source of true enlightenment.

In this vast ocean, in this sea of love,
You see nothing but love itself,
And what I usually call day
Seems like night when you know love.

Love so essentially pure is obscure to us,
For its light absorbs what lies without,
You cannot know or rationalize
What lies within this mystery.

No single object, but a deep gulf,
Lies roundabout our souls,
Which are lost and sometimes confounded
In a great sea of fire.

This fire is the very source of light
Yet it cannot wholly illuminate our mind.
It is not understood or described
Unless in terms that never comprehend it.

If you want to explain the ineffable,
It vanishes when you try to grasp it,
And the best approach to the light of light
Is not to speak but to be quiet.

For just to love, to love alone, is more joyful
Than any treatise or exposition, however long.
Now, dear heart, now and for ever,
Let us devote ourselves to silence full and deep.

'Océan du divin amour', from the divine poems of Madame Guyon; in
J. Mambrino, *La poésie mystique française*, Paris, 1973, pp. 58–9

HADEWIJCH

*In one of the poems which commentators still ascribe to her,
Hadewijch uses the language of courtly love for Christian ends.
This is a superb example of that highly emotional or ecstatic
spirituality of the period which held that the 'soul can only come
into contact with God by a love which makes it go out of itself,
which, indeed, drives it out of itself. This love is both joy and its
torment' (Dom François Vandenbroucke).*

Love of Christ

Ah! Dear Love, if any love I love,
'Tis Thee, my love.
Who givest grace for grace
The loved one to sustain.

4

Ah! Sweet Love, I would that I were love,
And loved thee, Love, with love itself!
Ah! Sweet Love, for love's sake grant
That love may wholly know her love.

Hadewijch, *Mengeldichten*, xv, in J. Leclercq et al., *The Spirituality of the Middle Ages*, London, 1968, p. 361

HILDEGARD OF BINGEN

Hildegard wrote to the Bishop of Bamberg to explain that love is the source and setting for all faith and purpose in life.

The power of love

The Father of us all is illumination, and illumination is both radiance and fire, clarity and inspiration, which are one and the same light. If you do not understand this in faith you do not see God for what he is, because you are trying to separate him from what he really is, and God is one: he cannot be divided. Even the works made by God lose their original meaning when human beings divide them up. This illumination is our Father's love, by which all things come into being and which surrounds all things, for all that is depends on the power of love. . . . Love is a fire that can never be put out. It is the vital source of the flames of true faith enlightening the hearts of real believers. Love of God sets them on fire with a faith they could never enjoy if they did not already love him in their hearts.

Analecta Sacra, Vol. 8, ed. J. B. Pitra, tr. J. Cumming, Monte Cassino, 1882, p. 400

JULIAN OF NORWICH

For Julian of Norwich, metaphor reaches deep into the ultimate meaning of things, and the supreme metaphor for ultimacy is motherhood. Julian asked God to help her understand Christ's sufferings, and came to understand that God answered her petition through her developing interpretation of divine love as motherly love. This concept reaches its daring high-point in her description of Christ becoming not man but woman in order to give birth to our salvation and, Julian seems to suggest, the ultimate redemption of all creation, without exception.

Mother and child

Our heavenly Mother is beautiful and delightful to our soul's eyes, and the children of grace are dear and beautiful in our heavenly Mother's eyes: they are gentle and humble, and have all the delightful natural attributes of children. A normal child never despairs of its mother's love, is never puffed-up, loves its mother, and loves other children. . . . I saw that childhood is the highest of all conditions in this life, because our abilities and minds are so unsatisfactory and weak until our gracious Mother lifts us up to enjoy our Father's happiness. Then we shall understand at last the real meaning of those wonderful words: 'All will be well. You will see for yourself now that everything will be all right.' Then the holy state of our motherhood in Christ will begin once again in the joys of our God, and there will be a new beginning that will last for ever. Then, through grace, all God's blessed children born to him by nature will live with him once again.

Revelation 14, BNF MS 40 Fonds Anglais

MECHTHILD OF MAGDEBURG

Mechthild experienced an intense love of God, 'who is my Father by his nature, my Brother by his humanity, and my Husband by his love'. Many years of this intensity led her to a highly nuanced understanding of the vagaries of love: 'I have learned something from suffering: anyone who is badly wounded by love will never recover unless she embraces the very same love that wounded her.' In her accounts of her visions, she tries to describe, in unusually original and wide-ranging imagery that shows her commonsense, and far from abstracted knowledge of human behaviour, how 'this God burning with desire' attracts a soul that is 'so very sick with love', until they are joined in a union that takes the soul through all human history, lifts her above everything ever known, yet then, paradoxically, demands total sacrifice, for it casts her down into the deepest gulf, until she is lower even than the souls in purgatory, the damned and Satan himself. Perhaps authentic love in all its mystery demands the risk of deepest depression, the experience of forsakenness by God. The following extended metaphor is typical of Mechthild's use of something in her surroundings (here, a fantastic animal in a mural painting or on a carved choir-stall) to portray some aspect of the human condition.

A spiritual person is like a certain animal

A depressed soul told her Lover sadly: 'Dear Lord, for a long time now I have wanted two things which I have never been given. One is an authentic spiritual life. Unfortunately, I have never been able to lead anything of the kind. The other is a holy death, although, when I think of that possibility with some assurance, my depression vanishes utterly.'

Our Lord replied by showing me a really tiny, unimportant creature. He said: 'Look! You're just like that little creature!' When I looked I saw how this creature was shaped from some slimy stuff on an island in the sea, and that it was trying to clean the slime away between the sun and the sea. Clearly, the sun was its father, the sea its mother, and the slime the stuff it was made from. This was how Adam was created from inferior stuff by God's power. The tiny creature stood for genuinely spiritual people. When human beings are given souls, they are conceived by the flaming Godhead, they receive the divine humanity in their mothers, and the stuff they are made of is the Holy Spirit, which gets rid of sinful nature in everything. This tiny creature develops in sunlight like any spiritual person who has been given God's spirit. The condition of any such creature is so propitious that it germinates and grows till the person reaches its final preordained and favourable state. A creature like this eats nothing but has a big tail packed with honey, which it sucks out every day. It has golden bristles which make so pleasing a sound when it is sucking its nourishment that the joyously sweet melody satisfies its heart while the honey contents its body. The creature's tail stands for the end of spiritual people, which they are continually aware of while they live doing never-failing good works and practising sound virtues, so that they are able to put up with their long wait without shirking. The creature's golden bristles symbolize God's loving kindness, the unforgettable sound of which penetrates the loving heart, and so resounds within it that it enters the soul. Human beings who were created in this way, and genuinely experience this, are truly blessed.

The creature always wants to drink from the sea because it is uncontrollably thirsty to an extent that it can never satisfy, yet it has to carry on drinking the bitter water and ejecting it. That's how it is with us sinners. Unfortunately, when we drink the world's muddy waters, and follow the evil spirit's advice on using our material senses, we merely poison ourselves. If we want to recover, we have to forget ourselves and reject worldly things.

The tiny creature has big ears, which it opens towards heaven. It hears the birds singing, runs away from wild beasts, and is afraid of earthly serpents. The loving soul lives in the same way, constantly avoiding evil company, abjuring phoney wisdom, and with its ears always open to receive God's wisdom.

This creature has a noble nature. It doesn't want to stay in the sea, where creatures fight and waters boil. Since it loves purity, it hurries up to the highest point it can reach to make its choices, and finds what is best there. It ascends joyfully and climbs the highest trees, where it takes its rest in love and complete freedom. Loving souls do the same, for they are well aware that virtuous behaviour and good works will enable them to climb to the very heights of the heavenly kingdom. Therefore, in grace, they effortlessly ascend the noblest tree of the holy Godhead. When they get there, they grasp the highest branch, where the Holy Trinity grasps them and holds them fast.

The creature has two sharp horns which it uses to defend its body so intelligently that it is protected from all wild beasts. I wish my soul could do exactly the same, for then God's own wisdom would enable you to drive the devil away, and you would live free of all sin.

The creature also has two beautiful human eyes which weep tears of longing for those vast mountains where it wishes to live. Loving soul, the eyes with which you contemplate these things are beautiful, because you have already peered into the mirror of eternity, and love has made sure that your tears are genuine. This means that you are ready to bear the bitter seas of sin without flinching.

The creature has a tender mouth and a clean tongue but no teeth, and it can't growl or bite. Loving human beings also have gentle mouths that allow them always to teach and judge happily, and to control their tongues and prevent them saying hurtful things. They have no biting teeth but are always prepared to comfort people who are depressed. They are only angry with sin and about contempt of God, which they find more painful than anything else.

The creature's mouth is wide at the top and narrow down below. We open our mouths most widely in order to praise God unstintingly together with all creatures, and in everything we do, at all times. Unfortunately the lower parts of our mouths are far too ready to talk about this sinful world. . . .

The creature is fleet of foot but has no voice. In itself, it is very quiet and self-contained, and the genuinely spiritual soul is the same, for when it truly loves it is quick to do so yet assured and still.

The creature's skin and hair are not impressive . . . and no one is greatly taken by its present beauty. After death, however, when other creatures decay, this creature's skin becomes so soft and rich that the highest people of all rely on it for their richest clothing. The world does not really prize the gentle lives of good people, their good behaviour and their spiritual wisdom, while they are alive. But, when we recall other people after death, we remember how holy their lives were and how truly they warned us. Then we are ashamed to think that we scarcely knew them. Then their lives become like the richest clothing, whose beauty we sinners admire, and are only too happy to wear in our hearts. . . .

When this creature is given a name, it means 'Everything that is good', for to those who love God, all things work together for good.

From Part IV of the *Revelations of Mechthild of Magdeburg*, tr. Lucy Menzies, London, 1953

MARGUERITE PORETE

Marguerite Porete, who refused to answer her interrogators in prison and was burnt at the stake for her obduracy in continuing to issue her book, presents the vision of plain truth which she considered she had the right to state in opposition, if necessary, to the Church's official teaching. Among her daring assertions was the metaphysical conceit that a truly loving soul wholly immersed in the immensity of God would dismiss even Christian virtues as irrelevant to absolutely pure love. The dialogue between Love and Reason is at the centre of the work.

Free souls are never burdened

Love: When these souls have come to love God as he is they are made conscious of their own nothingness – being nothing, having nothing, either from themselves, their fellow-Christians, or even from God himself. The soul is then so small she cannot see herself; all created things are so far from her she cannot feel them; God is so infinitely greater she cannot grasp him. Through this nothingness, she has the sureness of knowing nothing, being able to do nothing by herself, and willing nothing. And this nothingness brings her everything, which otherwise she would not have.

She is afloat on a sea of peace, drifting without any impulse from inside herself or any breeze from outside – both of which can undo peace, but not for her, because she is in full command and beyond interference or care. If she did anything through her outer senses, this would remain outside her, and if God did anything in her, this would be him working in her, for his own purpose, and so also outside her. What she does no more burdens her than what she does not do; she has no more being in herself, having given it all freely without asking 'why?'. She no longer feels doubt nor trust.

Reason: What does she feel, then?

Love: Absolute certainty, and total acceptance of the divine will; this is what makes her completely free.

The free soul lost in love

Being completely free, and in command on her sea of peace, the soul is nonetheless drowned and loses herself through God, with him and in him. She loses her identity, as does the water from a river – like the Ouse or the Meuse – when it flows into the sea. It has done its work and can relax in the arms of the sea, and the same is true of the soul. Her work is over and she can lose herself in what she has totally become: Love. Love is the bridegroom of her happiness enveloping her wholly in his love and making her part of that which is. This is a wonder to her and she has become a wonder. Love is her only delight and pleasure.

The soul now has no name but Union in Love. As the water that flows into the sea becomes sea, so does the soul become Love. Love and the soul are *no longer two things but one. She is then ready for the next stage.*

Reason: Can there be a next stage after this?

Love: Yes, once she has become totally free, she then falls into a trance of nothingness, and this is the next highest stage. Then she lives no longer in the life of grace, nor in the life of the spirit, but in the glorious life of divinity. God has conferred this special favour on her, and nothing except his goodness can now touch her.

May God grant you – those for whom Love has made this book, and for whom I have written it – to come to this life of being in him where there can be no change! But those who have not known this favour, and never will, will never understand it, try as they will. What it means is being in God without being oneself, since to be in God is being. But here the race is to the swift, and those who cannot swim in these waters will drown, and may drag others down with them.

Reason: Well put! Those who still have burdens tend to heap them on to other people's shoulders!

Charity and good works: Reason is shocked to death

Love: This soul is consumed in the flames of charity; her ashes are blown into the sea. Generous in good times, and even more so in bad, she is the essence of nobility in all she does.

The Soul: Her way to God is no longer through penances, nor the sacraments of the Church, nor thoughts nor words nor deeds. She is not helped on her way by creatures of this earth nor by those of heaven. She is beyond justice, mercy, glory, the knowledge and love of God, beyond praising his name.

Reason: Good God! What are you saying now? What am I or my followers supposed to make of this? I can't find any way of excusing a claim like this!

The Soul: Your brood have legs and cannot walk, hands and cannot work, mouths and cannot speak, eyes and cannot see, ears and cannot hear, reason and cannot think. Their bodies are lifeless and their minds dim. No wonder they are shocked!

Love: Yes, they must be amazed. They are far from the state in which these things can make sense to them. But those who live in the land of God have no trouble in understanding them.

The Soul: Think of it like this. If a king had a subject who had served him well, so well that he gave him a great gift which meant that he never had to work again for the rest of his life, would you blame the king for his generosity? No, why should anyone with any sense be shocked at this? My Beloved is the greatest king of all, and gives his great gifts freely to those he loves. So, those who are enlightened and fulfilled by the favour of his love have no further need of the consolations of this world. They can go direct to his peace.

Martha is troubled about many things; Mary is at peace. Martha is praiseworthy, but Mary more so. She has but one desire, and that brings her peace, whereas Martha has many concerns, and these cause conflict. So a free soul has only one desire. She hears what she cannot hear, exists where she cannot be, feels what she cannot feel. She holds on to this: he is with me, there is nothing I shall fear.

The Soul: With him, she is queen of virtues, daughter of the Godhead, sister of wisdom and bride of Love. Reason will wonder at such language, but he has reached his limit, whereas I was, am and shall be for evermore: love has no beginning or end, and is beyond understanding and I am pure love. How then can I ever end?

Reason: This is too much for me! I cannot bear it! My heart fails me and I am slain! (Dies)

The Soul: He should have died before. Now I can come freely into my own. The wound of love is the death of reason.

The soul's will is fixed in the Trinity

Love: This soul has no need to perform mundane tasks, because she lives in freedom. Those who have been truly caught up and captured and completely taken over by love, have no heart for anything but love, even if they have to suffer love's pangs and torments for ever, even though their sufferings are as great as God is good. Those who doubt this have not loved truly.

Charles Crawford, ed. and tr., *A Mirror for Simple Souls*, London, 1981, pp. 121–5

CHRISTINA ROSSETTI

Christina Rossetti's poems are often celebrated for their delicacy of feeling. She could also produce complex statements of insistent, yet thwarted, and indeed bloody, passion in which physical and devotional demands and apprehensions are intertwined and expressed through dream imagery, as the heart turns to dust and the hope of sexual fulfilment, 'like lead', crushes 'downwards through the sodden earth'.

I dreamed of you

For all night long I dreamed of you:
I woke and prayed against my will,
Then slept to dream of you again.
At length I rose and knelt and prayed;
I cannot write the words I said,
My words were slow my tears were few
But through the dark my silence spoke
Like thunder. When this morning broke,
My face was pinched, my hair was grey,
And frozen blood was on the sill
Where stifling in my struggle I lay.

From 'The Convent Threshold', in *Poetical Works of Christina Georgina Rossetti with Memoir and Notes etc.*, ed. William Michael Rossetti, London, 1935, p. 342

ST TERESA OF AVILA

Teresa of Avila could describe her experience of meeting God in richly original imagery that suggested the infinitely various ways in which he reveals himself to individuals, as when she portrayed the soul as a silkworm leaving its cocoon as a white butterfly; tried to convey the rapture of ultimate union with God at the very midpoint of the soul; or compared the life of prayer passing through phases of decreasing human effort to four methods of watering: a well, a water-wheel, a stream, and rain. She could also write with great simplicity, as when she wished to allay the anxiety of the nuns in her charge, and reassured them thus:

God alone suffices

Let nothing disturb you,
Nothing frighten you.
All things are transient.
God never changes.
Patience wins all things.
Who has God wants for nothing.
God alone suffices.

Silverio de Santa Teresa, ed., *Critical Edition of the Works of St Teresa of Avila* (in Spanish), vol. VI, Burgos, n.d., p. 127

SIMONE WEIL

Simone Weil wrestled with the paradox of God's apparent separation from his universe, and the signs of his presence in love and in the beauty of the world, which she represented as the body of the Soul of the world. This, in neo-Platonic terms, seemed somehow to precede not only the visible world but time. In complex language consonant with the profundity of her theme, and with the horror of twentieth-century suffering and devastation, she portrayed this body of the world's soul as the body of God's Son torn and suffering and cast into the wasteland of space and time where the soul must go on loving in emptiness.

Loving and waiting

Affliction makes God appear to be absent for a time, more absent than a dead man, more absent than light in the utter darkness of a cell. A kind of horror submerges the whole soul. During this absence there is nothing to love. What is terrible is that if, in this darkness where there is nothing to love, the soul ceases to love, God's absence becomes final. The soul has to go on loving in the emptiness, or at least to go on wanting to love, though it may only be with an infinitesimal part of itself. Then, one day, God will come to show himself to this soul and to reveal the beauty

of the world to it, as in the case of Job. But if the soul stops loving it falls, even in this life, into something almost equivalent to
hell. . . .

God created through love and for love. God did not create
anything except love itself, and the means to love. He created
love in all its forms. He created beings capable of love from all
possible distances. Because no other could do it, he himself went
to the greatest possible distance, the infinite distance. This infinite
distance between God and God, this supreme tearing apart, this
agony beyond all others, this marvel of love, is the crucifixion.
Nothing can be further from God than that which has been made
accursed.

This tearing apart, over which supreme love places the bond
of supreme union, echoes perpetually across the universe in the
midst of the silence, like two notes, separate yet melting into one,
like pure and heart-rending harmony. This is the Word of God.
The whole creation is nothing but its vibration. When human
music in its greatest purity pierces our soul, this is what we hear
through it. When we have learned to hear the silence, this is what
we grasp more distinctly through it.

The love between God and God, which in itself is God, is this
bond of double virtue: the bond that unites two beings so closely
that they are no longer distinguishable and really form a single
unity and the bond that stretches across distance and triumphs
over infinite separation. . . .

This universe where we are living, and of which we form a tiny
particle, is the distance put by Love between God and God. We
are a point in this distance. . . .

Simone Weil, *Waiting for God*; also in Edward Alcott, *A Great Treasury
of Christian Spirituality*, New York, 1978, pp. 118–25

Cosmic Christ and Natural World

❧

LUCIE CHRISTINE

Lucie Christine is a Christian of the modern age in seeing that even mystical ecstasy may be accompanied by doubt. She knows that an immovable assurance of God's love and everlasting presence may suddenly give way to dark uncertainty: 'This state of need and uncertainty seems as if it will never end. I am often tempted to deny any firm belief and trust, and give way to an irrational depression that has no meaning or purpose. At such times the presence of Jesus is almost entirely obscured.' Lucie Christine is also a modern woman in understanding not only that God as love urges us to love selflessly, but that the mysterious ability sometimes granted us to overcome deadly self-condemnation and self-hatred, to escape from overwhelming ego, depends on some kind of appreciation of God's incarnate mystery: that is, on an insight into his love as shown in his unselfish gift of himself and his beauty.

The beauty of God

Later in life, I realized that – without my being specifically aware of it – my spiritual longing for beauty and idealism had prepared me for the path that would eventually take me to God. . . . Indeed his first supernatural summons came as a surprise when it suddenly cast me directly into his arms. . . . Then my eyes opened and I began more than ever before to rejoice at your beauty, Lord, in sacred things. In the Gospels, in the psalms, and in the Church's rites and ceremonies, I discovered a divine meaning and

magic that had been relatively hidden from me until then. So I
focused on you alone the faculty to perceive and to admire which
you had given me. Then, wherever I found beauty I looked for
you, God, and so I found you everywhere. I questioned all created
things in a search for you and they all answered: 'Yes, he is here!'
I asked the sea where you were . . . and discovered that you rest
in its depths and cause life to course through its womb. I asked
its fissured coasts about you and from their proud heights they
replied: 'He is here!' I came upon you in the impenetrable shadows of the forests and I saw you pass over in the lightning. I met
you again in the distant wailing of the wind, in the rumble and
roar of thunder, and in the unleashed blustering of the stormy
air, and my heart was not afraid, for you were there. I greeted
you in the light of dawn and in the growing darkness of evening;
I surprised you in the cool valleys, and I listened to your voice in
the gentle murmurs of lonely streams. . . . I saw the face of your
mercy shine forth from the light of the stars above us, and I was
no longer frightened by their number and immeasurable distance,
for they invited me to flourish for ever in your eternity. . . .

Finally, I came to know you in your ultimate works, your saints;
I listened to the melody that reaches you through heroism, genius,
eloquence, scholarship, and the arts. Then I saw you, Jesus Christ
my Saviour, in the persons of the poor, old and troubled, who
bear the titles of nobility that you have given to all those who suffer and weep. I also looked for you in the strength, understanding
and achievements of youth and maturity, but because it hurt me
to find your sacred image so often disfigured or deformed, I went
ahead and searched elsewhere, and discovered you, Lord, in the
profundity of children's faces . . . for you are alive in souls that
have never saddened you, and you are that strange, secret force
that draws people towards the very fount of innocence, which
humankind is too weak to reach by its own efforts. There you
are, in the still unclouded gaze of childhood, dwelling within
souls untouched by evil. . . .

But then I experienced something extraordinary. Everything
which I had so admired up to that point was undeniably as beautiful as ever it had been, yet it no longer gave me the same degree

of joy. Just as the stars vanish in the light of the sun, so everything I had wondered at beforehand disappeared when God decided to look into my soul. Now I gazed at sea and land and saw nothing but God. Now, wherever I went, his drawing power increased, as did my resistance to everything other than God himself. Now, the result of this transformation is that, if nature reverts to its former condition and I feel an ordinary godless pleasure in anything, I am overcome by a profound psychological unease. I am deeply disturbed and feel a strange inner fear, as if I had been truly disloyal, and I just want to be rid of the pleasure I feel and to belong more surely to God than ever before. . . . Lord, you must tell me, I need to know. Is there any point in these outward expressions of inward joy and anguish, or should I restrain them? . . .

Yesterday when I took communion, my Lord appeared to me wrapped in a purple cloak that seemed to be decorated with flowers and jewels. I had no idea what this could mean, but Jesus said: 'You made it. It was you who put this cloak on me.' My astonished reply was: 'How on earth could I have done that, Lord? I haven't done anything at all for you.' All he said was: 'This cloak is love.' I think that by that he meant that it stood for the kind of love that loves and forgives irrespective of the fate that life decides to fasten on you. . . .

Journal spirituel, 6 May–13 November 1883, ed. P. A. Poulain SJ, Paris, 1916

MARGIAD EVANS

The Margiad Evans who wrote, 'Knowledge in me is like a peasant nun whose learning stopped at God and God alone' was able to draw poignant lessons from close observation of the natural world.

A great pastoral passion

Of Nature again . . . perhaps the discovery of God has undone my innocence. For there is no religious belief, no modern religious belief which at once contains and worships the earth, though most religions bid us watch the stars and consider their Maker, consider the sparrows and their Creator. Far from being able to watch the stars, religion (modern) will not have us bind our eyes to this one planet and its phenomena. I don't know therefore in what Faith I could enclose my solitary response to ordinary common Nature, unless within the ancient Jewish faith or the great Symbolical plurality of the old Greeks. That is, what is known to me of either. Of the old Jewish faith, as disclosed in the Old Testament, it seems clear by description and implication, that a great pastoral passion was enclosed within it . . . , so illuminated is every historical, prophetic and poetic Book by the imagery of an old people whose every ultimate idea of beauty, peace and benignity was conveyed by illustrations from the beautiful in Nature.

Margiad Evans, *A Ray of Darkness*, London, 1952, pp. 91–2

ANN GRIFFITHS

The Cosmic Christ

Ann Griffiths is conscious of the entirely paradoxical yet utterly compelling nature of the joining of God and humankind in one Person, Christ. She understands its relevance to her own being and prayer-life because she is also aware of the connection between this mysterious contradiction and the further paradox that Christ's death is the means by which life is given to all humankind. Her vision is individual and cosmic, for she sees the utter devotion of Christ's acceptance from all eternity of the part he must play. This insight is strengthened by one of the most profound emphases of Calvinism: that placed on the affirmation that Christ's living and dying glorify God by fulfilling eternal law and justice. She presents this as our assurance that there is meaning in human life and in the universe, and in the very ardour of her verse this conviction appears as irrefutable truth.

Against the grain

(Er mai cwbwl groes i natur / Yw fy llwybyr yn y byd)

You know, Lord, that the way I must take
  runs against the grain of the person I am.
All the same, I'll keep on it
  as long as I can see your face.
If I can look at you, I'll stay calm and unflinching.
I'll carry the cross they've got ready for me,
I'll even think of it as a crown, and be cheerful
  in spite of this life's gross miseries,
  and so many harsh disappointments.

Certainly, the road I am on has
  a great many obstacles and entanglements.
All the same, there's no doubt where it leads:
  straight to the city of true happiness.

It is the way called wonderful,
  the way that's old yet ever new,
  never beginning, never aging,
  where the dead will live again;
It is the way that's irresistible
  to all who take it,

It is a road that's husband,
  a way that's head,
  a way that's holy,
It is the road I'll follow,
  and on it, in it, rest for ever.

No sharp-eyed predator can pick it out,
  however bright and clear it blazes.
No one can see or take it
  unless faith clears her sight.

It is the way of God's own justice
  and his everlasting law.
It is the way that justifies the godless,
  the way that calls the dead to rise.
It leads lost souls to God's own kindness,
  his forgiveness and his loving peace.

The road I'm on was planned
  with us in mind.
Each detail was prepared
  before we were summoned here,
  and every inch designed
  to fit our needs.

When God foresaw the great calamity
  at the beginning of all time,
  he made a new agreement.
He gave us the cup of true hope:
  the chalice of new wine
  by which our love and courage are refreshed,
  and his own heart is filled with joy.

Translated by John Griffiths

HILDEGARD OF BINGEN

For Hildegard the love of God is a splendid winged figure whose face is illuminated by beauty and clarity.

I, the fiery life of divine essence, flame out over the beauty of the fields, shine in the waters, and burn in the sun, moon, and stars. With every breath of air I awaken all things to life. The air comes alive as nature grows green and blooms, and the waters flow as if they too were alive. The sun blazes as a living light, and the moon is kindled and constantly renewed by the sun's fire. For love is life. It is life whole and entire, not struck from stones, not

22

blossoming from branches, and not rooted in human generative power.

H. Schipperges, *The World of Hildegard of Bingen: Her Life, Times and Visions*, tr. J. Cumming, London, 1997, p. 68

Holy Wisdom

Holy Wisdom in your power
Hold us fast in every hour.

Enclose us in your threefold wings
Spreading to embrace all things.

One pierces heaven's heights above,
Another touches earth with love.

The other moves with tender care
In mystery through the cosmic air.

Holy Wisdom in your power
Enlighten us in every hour.

Schipperges, *The World of Hildegard of Bingen*, p. 73

RAÏSSA MARITAIN

Among the major themes of Raïssa Maritain's journal and poetry are the affective beauty of Creation as a sign of God's handiwork, the soul's desire for union with God, and the sense of deprivation and exile experienced by a mystical personality forced to lead a material existence. Throughout her writing life she tried to make the reader feel something of God's extraordinary presence in people, things and thought, as in this poem.

The world's mellow tenderness

Mellow tenderness of this world! Your music resounds as it rises and falls in my heart, and your magic is ours for ever.

One hour at the heart of your beauty, one earthly, one real hour: blessing without past, present without future, in your all-embracing love.

Wonders of springtime, everlasting garden of delights, the sky is bright and clear, and a gentle light seems to descend from paradise.

Flowering branches of acacias, orange trees, roses and lilacs: a fullness of growth among miraculously fruitful trees.

Look! There the wood and tree of the Cross bear his Flower and everlasting Fruit!

The heart is more fertile even than any tree. Its fruit matures in silence; its blood-rich grape awaits the press.

Fragile and carnal vessel, secret and open universe where the world's tenderness flows with blood.

O soft sweetness! O fullness! O joy! So many words and exclamations are yours.

You speak only through the hidden beating of this heart which only the angels of music can interpret and proclaim.

My enthusiasm has explored the earth and the sky. I have seemed to possess all there is to know in these everlasting moments.

These happy moments and this privileged hour have gathered up all the separate, scattered instances of love in the world.

This is the most perfect of hours, an hour which the gods themselves envy. An hour which perhaps even God himself defends jealously and which we must yield up to him whole and entire, with the greatest care.

If you hear his voice today, do not close your ears to the sound.

Come, we must go now: this is the testing time, for Jacob's ladder is laid against our heart.

Come, let us go, and abandon even beauty itself for God's sweet sake, for he holds the whole star-studded universe in his tender hand.

Let us go. Let us collect ourselves, and call to order our forgetful hearts, that were so intent on abandoning all thought of God to live without him among all he has made.

Let us weep before the God who made us, and from whom all that is good comes to us: all humility, all gentleness and all pure teardrops.

Let us go, all together in a flock, and bear our delights and our pleasures on the same path of pain where he must carry his cross.

This is the road which he has dared to take before us: Isaac the humble, burdened with the wood of sacrifice.

Jesus wishes us to die so that we may have life, so do not be afraid: you may be fearful in the Garden of Olives.

Jesus will feed us with joy from living springs, so do not be afraid. All is well, you may go now and die with him.

R. Maritain, *Poèmes et Essais*, Paris, 1968; also in J. Mambrino, *La poésie mystique française*, Paris, 1973, pp. 192–3

ALICE MEYNELL

Alice Meynell conveys intense religious feeling by choice of words and by subtle melody as she tackles the very modern notion of millions of forms of God in millions of worlds.

Christ in the universe

With this ambiguous earth
His dealings have been told us. These abide:
The signal to a maid, the human birth,
The lesson, and the young Man crucified.

But not a star of all
The innumerable host of stars has heard
How he administered this terrestrial ball.
Our race have kept their Lord's entrusted Word.

Of his earth-visiting feet
None knows the secret, cherished, perilous
The terrible, shame fast, frightened, whispered, sweet,
Heart-shattering secret of his way with us.

No planet knows that this
Our wayside planet, carrying land and wave,
Love and life multiplied, and pain and bliss,
Bears, as chief treasure, one forsaken grave.

Nor, in our little day,
May his devices with the heavens be guessed,
His pilgrimage to thread the Milky Way,
Or his bestowals there be manifest.

But, in the eternities,
Doubtless we shall compare together, hear
A million alien Gospels, in what guise
He trod the Pleiades, the Lyre, the Bear.

O be prepared, my soul!
To read the inconceivable, to scan
The million forms of God those stars unroll
When, in our turn, we show to them a Man.

Alice Meynell, *Poems*, ed. F. Meynell, London, 1947; also in *The New Oxford Book of English Verse*, ed. Helen Gardner, Oxford, 1972, p. 791

ST EDITH STEIN

Someone who attended a lecture by Edith Stein in 1930, when she spoke extempore for two hours, wrote that 'a restrained dynamic was contained in every sentence. I cannot remember having felt tired for even one minute. For here one sensed a great power of mind, a rich, yet disciplined inner life, born of utmost self-assurance.' This is evident in all the statements on the individual and the universal of this saint who knew that: 'We always have our neighbour before us and it is always our neighbour who has the greatest call on us. The love of Christ knows no frontiers.'

The great development of humanity

[E]ach individual has his place and task in the one great development of humanity. Humanity is to be understood as one great individual; it is possible to understand salvation history only by this interpretation. Each person is a member of this whole, and the essential structure of the whole is shown in every member; but, at the same time, each has his own character as a member of which he must develop if the whole is to attain development. The species *humanity* is realized perfectly only in the course of world history in which the great individual, humanity, becomes concrete.

Essays on Women, Collected Works of Edith Stein, vol. II, p. 189; also in Sarah Borden, *Edith Stein*, London, 2003, p. 121

ST THÉRÈSE OF LISIEUX

Thérèse of Lisieux puzzles out the paradoxical nature of God's creation and restates her understanding of it in metaphorical terms.

Undeserved favours

I have often asked myself why God has preferences, and doesn't give all souls an equal amount of grace. . . . But Jesus graciously explained this mystery to me. He showed me the book of nature. Then I understood that every flower he has made is beautiful: how the rose's brilliance and lily's whiteness don't reduce the little violet's perfume or the daisy's lovely simplicity. I saw that if all the lesser flowers wanted to be roses, nature would lose its springtime beauty, and the fields would no longer be patterned with the hues of little flowers. It is the same in the world of souls, which is Jesus' garden. He wanted to make great saints who may be compared to lilies and roses, but he has also created lesser ones; and these lesser ones must be content to rank as daisies and violets, flower at his feet and gladden his eyes when he looks down at them, for perfection means doing his will, being what he wants us to be. . . .

I also understood that our Lord's love is shown to us as much in the simplest soul that does not resist his grace as in the most highly endowed. In fact, since the nature of love is to make yourself small, if all souls resembled the holy Doctors who have illumined the Church . . . it would seem as if God weren't stooping low enough when he came into *their* hearts. But he has created little children, who know nothing about anything and can only make themselves heard by feeble crying; and he has made the poor savages, who have only the natural law to follow; and it is to their hearts that he is willing to come down. These are the wild flowers whose simplicity charms him, and it is by his condescension to them that God shows his infinite greatness. The same sun's light that shines on the cedar-tree shines uniquely on the smallest flower. Just so, our Lord concentrates on each soul uniquely, and everything works together for the good of each soul, just as in nature the seasons are arranged to ensure that the humblest daisy will unfold its petals on the appointed day. . . .

If a little flower could talk, I think it would say quite simply what God has done for it, and not hide any of his gifts. It wouldn't say, in mock humility, that it wasn't pretty and didn't smell sweet, that the sun had withered its petals or a storm bruised its stem, if it knew all that wasn't true. The flower now telling her tale is delighted to record our Lord's wholly undeserved favours. She knows that in herself she had nothing that could have drawn his attention, for it was his mercy that put anything good in her–his mercy alone.

He decided that she was to be born in holy ground fragrant with the scent of purity. He made sure that eight dazzling white lilies sprang up there before she appeared. He loved his little flower so much that he wanted to protect her from the poisoned air of the world, for her petals had hardly unfolded when her divine Master transplanted her to Mount Carmel. . . .

Thérèse de l'Enfant-Jésus et de La Sainte Face, Histoire d'une Âme, Lisieux, 1898; rev. ed., Lisieux, c. 1915; *Oeuvres Complètes*, pp. 71–4; also in Felicity Leng, *Smiles of God: The Flowers of St Thérèse of Lisieux,* London, 2003, pp. 6–7

Creativity and Visions

܀

ST BERNADETTE OF LOURDES

Bernadette Soubirous, who spoke no French but only the patois peculiar to the Lourdes area, with a very limited vocabulary (the same language used by her visitant), described her first vision of Mary in very straightforward terms. In spite of all attempts by religious, priests, and the sculptor commissioned to reproduce her vision to make her remember a visitation by a much taller, older and more elaborately clothed lady, she insisted that the person who had suddenly appeared before her fourteen-year-old self was a very young girl of about twelve, no taller than Bernadette herself.

An unexpected vision

I had scarcely left the foot of the hill when I heard the wind blowing as if a storm was coming up. It seemed to be coming from all the neighbouring slopes and to move in every direction. I turned towards the side where there was a field and saw that the trees were quite still. I did catch a glimpse, though I did not fix my gaze on this, of branches and brambles stirring on the side of the grotto.

I finished taking off my stockings and dipped my foot in the water, when I heard the same sound in front of me. I raised my eyes and saw a cluster of branches and brambles stirring to and fro, below the highest opening of the grotto, although nothing was moving round that part.

Then, immediately afterwards, in the opening I saw a young girl dressed in white. She was no taller than me. She greeted me with a slight nod, and at the same time stretched her arms out a little from her body, opening her hands as in statues of the Holy Virgin. A rosary hung from her right arm.

I was afraid and drew back. I wanted to call the two little children, but I was too frightened. I rubbed my eyes several times, because I thought I was imagining it.

When I raised my eyes again I saw the young girl smiling very kindly and seeming to ask me to come over to her. But I was still afraid. It wasn't the same kind of fear I've experienced on other occasions, because I would always stay to see her, whereas, when you're afraid, you get going very quickly.

Then I thought of praying. I put my hand in my pocket. I took out the rosary that I usually carry around. I kneeled down and tried to make the sign of the cross, but I couldn't get my hand up to my forehead; it just fell back again.

Meanwhile the girl stood to one side and turned towards me. This time she was holding her big rosary in one hand. She made the sign of the cross, as if she was about to pray. My hand shook. Once again I tried to bless myself, and this time I succeeded. After that I wasn't afraid.

I said the rosary. The girl passed the beads of her rosary between her fingers, but her lips did not move.

While saying my rosary I looked at her as much as I could.

She was wearing a white dress. It fell right down to her feet, so that I could see no more than the tips of them. Very high up, around her neck, the dress was fastened by a hem from which a white cord emerged. A white veil covered her head and fell over her shoulders and arms, covering her almost to the bottom of her dress. I saw a yellow rose on each of her feet. Her sash was blue and hung lower than her knees. The rosary had a yellow chain. The beads were big, white and strung at some distance from each other.

The girl was very young, lively and clothed in light.

When I had finished my rosary she smiled at me. She went back into the niche and suddenly disappeared.

Francis Trochu, *Sainte Bernadette*, Paris, 1954, pp. 81–3

ST CATHERINE OF GENOA

Catherine of Genoa's account of her self-contemplation in a state of spiritual schizophrenia has many counterparts in mystics' and others' accounts of out-of-the-body experiences which they have been granted after extreme physical or mental suffering, or during comas.

Suspended in mid-air

One day (she said) she appeared to herself to abide suspended in mid-air. And the spiritual part wanted to attach itself to heaven; but her other part wished to attach itself to earth: yet neither the one nor the other managed to become possessed of its object, and simply abode thus in mid-air, without achieving its desire. And after abiding thus for a long time, the part which was drawing her to heaven seemed to her to be gaining the upper hand (over the other part), and, little by little, the spiritual part forcibly drew her upwards, so that at every moment she saw herself moving further and further away from earth. And although this at first seemed to be a strange thing to the part that was being drawn, and this part was ill content to be thus forced; yet when it had been so far removed, as no more to be able to see the earth, then it began to lose its earthly instinct and affection, and to perceive and to relish the things which were relished by the spiritual part. And this spiritual part never ceased from drawing it heavenward. And so at last these two parts came to a common accord. And again on another occasion: The soul is so desirous of departing from the body to unite itself with God, that its body appears to it a veritable Purgatory, which keeps it distant from its true object.

Friedrich von Hügel, *The Mystical Element of Religion as Studied in Saint Catherine of Genoa and Her Friends*, vol. I, London, 1908, pp. 189–90

MARGIAD EVANS

Margiad Evans was able to express most memorably her insight into the multiple layers of the human spirit.

Profundity on profundity

To and fro over the expanse of fields and trees and streams, led from sound to sound – led by sound up into the air and down below the level of the earth to where the snakes are sleeping with their eyes glazed, consciousness roams while one's body rests in an unconsciousness even of existence. All that one sees and hears exists and is beautiful, mysterious, full of meaning. Far away with the bees in their cells, yet one hears and loves the elms uttering the wind, the nearby blue-tits hopping round and round, blurs of green and yellow and blue mixed by movement like the colours on a top. All is simultaneous. Therein lives the uncommunicable wonder, the difficulty of writing. The hues, the sun, the living-ness in the eye, that which is in the mind and that which lives around and is seen, they are all simultaneous. Consciousness has many layers, profundity on profundity. For this one and separate miracles, the universe, the now, substitute words which must be added one after another, and the vision finishes as a list.

Margiad Evans, *Autobiography*, London, 1943, p. 75

ST GERTRUDE OF HELFTA

Gertrude of Helfta describes her joyous vision of intense union with Jesus and his heart as a wound in her heart caused by a ray of light darting from his side, granted as a pledge of his love.

A ray of sunshine

When, after receiving the life-giving sacrament, I had come back to my place of prayer, it seemed to me as though there came forth from the crucifix depicted in my book (that is, from the wound in the side) something like a ray of sunshine, in the likeness of a sharpened arrow. It appeared first to stretch forth, then to contract itself and then to stretch forth again, and continuing thus for a time, it sweetly drew my affection to itself.

St Gertrude of Helfta, *Legatus*, II, 5; see Leclercq et al., *The Spirituality of the Middle Ages*, London, 1968, p. 453

IDA GÖRRES

Ida Görres wrote some of her most effective prose in the period following a severe illness during which, as in this short commentary on the contemporary implications of two well-known parables, she questioned the extent and limits of human abilities and purpose.

The very tiniest beginnings

The grain of mustard seed and the leaven once again. The Kingdom of Heaven can take root and sprout up in a human heart from the very tiniest beginnings, virtually without human assistance (the mustard seed was probably never sown on purpose, but dropped by a bird or blown by the wind) – yet it really took root, grew into a 'tree', sturdy and enduring, steadfast in all weathers, and the birds of the air (divine inspirations, etc.) can really nest in its branches. But it's 'in the garden' for all that, in a cultivated demesne, i.e. man must do something himself – at least keep the soil raked and hoed, so that a chance seed blown by the wind can settle and be nourished.

The leaven: 'We prefer our yeast pure' [they say], meaning Catholic piety in the form we all know – instead of mixing it with the flour of the world around us, of ordinary everyday life, and letting these three measures of meal be leavened. We're so afraid of spoiling the yeast by taking it out of its nice hygienic little cellophane packet and breaking it up, stirring and mixing, past recognition. And then you must remember to set the dough aside to rise, leaving it to itself for a while, else nothing will happen at all! Both parables stress the insignificance of beginnings. One must have the courage to scatter even the tiniest, most inconspicuous, unheeded suggestions at random, leaving it to God to make what he will of them – if anything.

Ida Friederike Görres, *Broken Lights*, tr. B. Waldstein-Wartenberg, London, 1964, pp. 84–5

HILDEGARD OF BINGEN

For Hildegard, God is the ultimate artist continually remaking and illuminating his special creation, human beings. They are his apprentices and collaborators, and follow his blueprints within their souls, the workshops where he teaches them how to work out their destinies. He makes the world as an architect lays out a garden:

A master who wants to design a garden most proficiently first of all finds a suitable site. Then, if he wants to be both a great philosopher and an expert craftsman, he finds the right place for each variety, and considers the fruitfulness and utility of different kinds of trees and vegetables, chooses the really good ones, and plants them. Then he erects a protective wall around his garden and appoints an under-gardener who knows how to water the site, collect the fruits of the various plants, and make different remedies from them.

Scivias I, 2 in *Patrologia Latina*, Vol. 197, tr. J. Cumming, Paris, 1882, cc. 383–78

When Hildegard was sixty-five she had a visionary experience, an encounter with what she called the 'Living Light', when her 'bodily senses were annulled and my perception was wholly transformed, as though I no longer knew who I was! And my conscious mind received what seemed to be gentle drops of rain trickling from the imagination of God.' Over seven years she wrote, as if by dictation from a higher source, De operatione Dei *(The*

Book of Divine Works*), her cosmological work that reveals the mysterious links between human beings, the world, and God.*

The living light

I am always beset by fear and trembling, since I am not at all confident in my own abilities, but stretch out my hands to God so that he can hold me like a feather weighing nothing and subject to the wind's power. . . . I do not see these things with my outward vision or listen to them with my outward hearing. I see them only within, yet with my outer eyes open, so that I never become unconscious as in an ecstasy. I am fully awake when I see all this, by day and by night. The light I see is not confined by space. It is lighter and brighter than a cloud carrying the sun. This light has neither height, nor length, nor breadth. I am told that it is the 'shadow of the living light'.

What I see and learn in these visions I keep in my memory for a long time, so that when I see and hear this light I remember and simultaneously see, hear, and understand, as it were in that very instant, what I then know.

But what I do not see I do not know or understand, because I am no scholar. . . . In this light I sometimes see another light that I am told is 'the living light'. When and how I see it I cannot say. But while I see it I am quite without sorrow and anxiety, so that I feel like a young girl and not like an old woman.

Analecta Sacra, Vol. 8, ed. J. B. Pitra, tr. J. Cumming, Monte Cassino, 1882, pp. 332–3

In a vision she describes in her Scivias *(Know the Ways), Hildegard encounters the figure of the Church. She explains how the foundations of the eternal dwelling-places of a wholesome world are made ready on this earth.*

A wholesome world

After this I saw the vision of a tall woman. She was as imposing as a great city and had a wonderful and beautifully decorated crown on her head. A lustrous shower of extraordinary brilliance descended from her arms almost like sleeves shimmering and shining from heaven to earth. Her womb was like a giant net with many apertures through which a great throng of people passed. I could not see any clothing on this woman, but she was entirely suffused with a brilliant light and totally enclosed in gleaming splendour. Daybreak glowed and glistened on her breast, and from everywhere about her I heard that sparkling dawn singing a glorious medley of tunes of every kind.

This figure radiated such splendour that it seemed to flow about her like a garment. As I looked, she began to speak: 'I must conceive and give birth!' Immediately a band of angels hastened toward her. They prepared steps and seats in her for all the people who would bring the figure to perfection. Then I saw a great number of little children close to the ground swimming through the air like fishes in water. They made their way through the openings in the figure and entered her womb. She drew her breath in sharply and pulled them up to her head, whereupon they flew out of her mouth. So she remained quite unharmed by them.

Scivias II, 3 in *Patrologia Latina*, Vol. 197, tr. J. Cumming, Paris, 1882, cc. 383–78

EMILY DICKINSON

Emily Dickinson's poem points up the ironies of striving and salvation.

A poor – torn heart – a tattered heart –
That sat it down to rest –
Nor noticed that the Ebbing Day
Flowed silver to the West –
Nor noticed Night did soft descend –
Nor Constellation burn –

Intent upon the vision
Of latitudes unknown.

The angels – happening that way
This dusty heart espied –
Tenderly took it up from toil
And carried it to God –
There – sandals for the Barefoot –
There – gathered from the gales –
Do the blue havens by the hand
Lead the wandering Sails.

The Complete Poems of Emily Dickinson, ed. Thomas H. Johnson, London, 1970, p. 40

JULIAN OF NORWICH

Julian of Norwich describes her visions with the graphic exactitude found in devotional wood-carving of the period. She portrays events of cosmic importance in homely terms that remind us that the redemption of the universe is involved in its every aspect, even the look and sound of raindrops falling from a gutter, or the appearance of fish-scales.

Fresh and credible

I thought I could see his head continually bleeding, and that with my real, outward eyes. Vast round drops of blood like beads rolled down from the garland round his head, reddish-brown drops issuing from his veins it seemed, and turning bright red as they flattened out, then disappearing on reaching his eyebrows. This bleeding went on as long as I had to see and understand anything. The drops were as fresh and credible as if they were real. There were as many of them as the drops that fall from the eaves of a house after heavy rain, and came down so thick and fast that no one could ever count them. They looked like round herring scales as they spread out on his forehead. . . . I was comforted to know that our Lord God is so caring and unpretentious.

Revelation 7, BNF MS 40 Fonds Anglais

MARGERY KEMPE

Margery Kempe's account of the sight and sound of the divine Presence is one of the most singular yet attractive ever written.

Wheresoever God is heaven is

She saw with her bodily eyes many white things flying all about her on every side as thick as motes in a sunbeam. They were minute and pleasant to see, and the brighter the sun shone, the better could she see them. She saw them many different times and in many different places, both in church and in her room, at her meat and in her prayers, in field and in town, both walking and sitting. And many times she was afeard what they might be, for she saw them as well at night in darkness as in daylight. Then, when she was afeared of them, our Lord said to her, 'By this token, daughter, believe it is God that speaketh in thee, for wheresoever God is heaven is, and where God is there be many angels, and God is in thee and thou art in him. And therefore be not afeared, daughter, for these betoken that thou hast many angels about thee to keep thee both night and day that no devil shall have power over thee, nor evil man to harm them'. Then from that time forward she used to say when she saw them coming: 'Benedictus qui venit in nomine Domini' [Blessed who cometh in the name of the Lord].

. . . This creature had divers tokens in her bodily hearing. One was a kind of sound as if it had been a pair of bellows blowing in her ear. She, being startled thereat, was warned in her soul to have no fear, for it was the sound of the Holy Ghost. And then our Lord turned that sound into the voice of a dove, and then he turned it into the voice of a little bird which is called a redbreast that sang full merrily oftentimes in her right ear.

The Book of Margery Kempe, as cited by David Knowles, *The English Mystical Tradition*, London, 1961, pp. 145–6

MARIE LATASTE

The poet Coventry Patmore wrote of Marie Lataste: 'Her life was all grace and miracle, and her writings full of living sanctity and vigorous perceptions of things hidden to the wise. There are no such books in English, but many in French.' She became Psyche in his major poem 'The Unknown Eros'. Her account of a conversation with her angel guardian reflects priestly admonitions common in the French church at the time, but also her ability to represent spiritual things graphically.

The beast and the cross

My angel guardian came to keep me company and converse with me. . . . 'I have brought you a cross; hold firmly by the chain you have in your hand; an attempt will be made to detach you from it, but with the cross you will repulse all who approach you.' I took the cross which my angel presented to me.

Immediately the sand was lifted up, and a huge beast, such as I had never beheld before, issued from underground and came and lay before me, two or three steps off, for the space was very narrow. Its body was as big as that of an ox, but the legs were shorter; its head also was like the head of an ox. It had several horns, large and small; its eyes resembled those of an ox; its mouth was very wide, out of which came a tongue of excessive length, ending in two very sharp points. On its back it bore a town, in which I saw nothing but dancing-halls and theatres. It hurled at me darts, lances, and balls, which I drove back with my cross, and they rebounded and wounded it. Soon there came a great multitude of assailants in the form of men. They were very small, and appeared to me to be very nimble. They careered and wheeled around me; when they got near me I confronted them with my cross and they retreated. They disappeared and were replaced by other men, taller than the first. These endeavoured to wrest the golden chain from my hand, but I repulsed them victoriously by presenting my cross at them. They made a last effort, and tried to throw me down, but my cross put them to flight.

While combating these adversaries I did not lose sight of the beast before me. I saw it bring its head stealthily near me to pierce me with its horns or its tongue; I struck it with my cross, and the men and the beast ceased attacking me. The men disappeared, but a vast number of crows swooped down upon me, trying to peck out my eyes. Unable to defend myself alone, I pulled at the chain and cried aloud to the Saviour Jesus. Immediately a shower of leaden hailstones came down upon them, and laid them dead at my feet.

Letters and Writings of Marie Lataste, tr. Edward Healy Thompson
vol. 1, London, 1894, pp. 352–3

ST TERESA OF AVILA

After hearing Teresa of Avila talk joyously of our Lord, Ana de San Bartolomé, a lay sister, told her sisters in God: 'You are like angels, but the Mother Foundress is a seraphim aflame with the love of God and her neighbour.' Teresa was noted for her unique descriptions of her spiritual experiences, as when she struggled to define the unusual nature of the vision of Christ that she had been vouchsafed without requesting or expecting it.

Visions and words

I went to my confessor, in great distress. . . . He asked in what form I saw our Lord. I told him I saw no form. He then said: 'How did you know that it was Christ?' I replied, that I did not know how I knew it; but I could not help knowing that Christ was close beside me – that I saw him distinctly, and felt his presence. . . .

If I say that I see him neither with the eyes of the body, nor with those of the soul – because it was not an imaginary vision – how is it that I can understand and maintain that he stands beside me, and be more certain of it than if I saw him? If it be supposed that it is as if a person were blind, or in the dark, and therefore unable to see another who is close to him, the comparison is not exact. There is a certain likelihood about it, however, but not much, because the other senses tell him who is blind of that presence:

he hears the other speak or move, or he touches him; but in these visions there is nothing like this. The darkness is not felt; only he renders himself present to the soul by a certain knowledge of himself which is more clear than the sun. I do not mean that we now see either a sun or any brightness, only that there is a light not seen, which illumines the understanding so that the soul may have the fruition of so great a good. This vision brings with it great blessings.

It is not like that presence of God which is frequently felt, particularly by those who have attained to the prayer of union and of quiet, when we seem, at the very commencement of our prayer, to find him with whom we would converse, and when we seem to feel that he hears us by the effects and the spiritual impressions of great love and faith of which we are then conscious, as well as by the good resolutions, accompanied by sweetness, which we then make. This is a great grace from God; and let him to whom he has given it esteem it much, because it is a very high degree of prayer; but it is not vision. God is understood to be present there by the effects he works in the soul: that is the way his Majesty makes his presence felt; but here, in this vision, it is seen clearly that Jesus Christ is present, the Son of the Virgin. In the prayer of union and of quiet, certain inflowings of the Godhead are present; but in the vision, the sacred Humanity also, together with them, is pleased to be our visible companion, and to do us good.

My confessor next asked me, who told me it was Jesus Christ, I replied, that he often told me so himself; but, even before he told me so, there was an impression on my understanding that it was he; and before this he used to tell me so, and I saw him not. If a person whom I had never seen, but of whom I had heard, came to speak to me, and I were blind, or in the dark, and told me who he was, I should believe him; but I could not so confidently affirm that he was that person, as I might do if I had seen him. But in this vision I could do so, because so clear a knowledge is impressed on the soul that all doubt seems impossible, though he is not seen. Our Lord wills that this knowledge be so graven on the understanding, that we can no more question his presence than we can question that which we see with our eyes: not so much even; for very often there arises a suspicion that we have imagined things we think we see: but here, though there may be a suspicion in the first instant, there remains a certainty so great, that the doubt has no force whatever. So also is it when God teaches the soul in another way, and speaks to it without speaking, in the way I have described.

There is so much of heaven in this language, that it cannot well be understood on earth, though we may desire ever so much to explain it, if our Lord will not teach it experimentally. Our Lord impresses in the innermost soul that which he wills that soul to understand; and he manifests it there without images or formal words, after the manner of the vision I am speaking of. Consider well this way in which God works, in order that the soul may understand what he means – his great truths and mysteries; for very often what I understand, when our Lord explains to me the vision which it is his Majesty's pleasure to set before me, is after this manner; and it seems to me that this is a state with which the devil can least interfere, for these reasons; but if these reasons are not good, I must be under a delusion. The vision and the language are matters of such pure spirituality, that there is no turmoil of the faculties, or of the senses, out of which – it seems to me – the devil can derive any advantage.

It is only at intervals, and for an instant, that this occurs; for generally – so I think – the senses are not taken away, and the faculties are not suspended: they preserve their ordinary state. It is not always so in contemplation; on the contrary, it is very rarely so; but when it is so, I say that we do nothing whatever ourselves: no work of ours is then possible; all that is done is apparently the work of our Lord. It is as if food had been received into the stomach which had not first been eaten and without our knowing how it entered; but we do know well that it is there, though we know not its nature, nor who it was that placed it there. In this vision, I know who placed it; but I do not know how he did it. I neither saw it, nor felt it; I never had any inclination to desire it, and I never knew before that such a thing was possible.

The Life of St Teresa of Avila by Herself, tr. David Lewis, ed. D. Knowles, London, 1962, pp. 198–201.

ST THÉRÈSE OF LISIEUX

*Thérèse wrote the following poem as part of a dramatic piece for
Christmas 1894. She attributed the words to an angel of the Child
Jesus. Thérèse was known as the 'Little Flower', and identified
flowers with souls here, and even more explicitly when she wrote
more metaphorically, as in the prologue to Manuscript A of her
autobiography.*

A smile of God

A flower is a smile of God,
A distant echo of heaven,
A single, fleeting note
Of God's own music,
A perfectly-formed note
In his all-making harmony,
A voice full of mystery, dear Saviour,
That sings of your great power:
   Infinitely melodious,
   Sweetly harmonious
Silence of flowers,
Telling God in his grandeur.

These flowers that we love so,
Jesus, I know, are your friends,
For you come from heavenly meadows
To find your sisters, the flowers,
Holy Child, I know you are eager
To gather our fragrant souls.
Dear Jesus, Lily of the Valley,
There is nothing you would not give
For one of us, your flowers.
   Mystery beyond words,
   Word of words, our Beloved,
You must weep still
As you take up your harvest of flowers.

Author's translation of 'Les Anges à la Crèche de Jésus', cf. *Histoire d'une Âme*, Lisieux, 1898 and 'Récréations pieuses', 25 December 1894, in *Oeuvres Complètes*, Paris, 2001, p. 801; also in Felicity Leng, *Smiles of God: the Flowers of St Thérèse of Lisieux*, London, 2003, pp. 1–2

EVELYN UNDERHILL

Something of the quality of Evelyn Underhill's inventiveness in her addresses, which made her so popular a speaker, is apparent in this fairy story:

One needful thing

I read the other day the story of a brownie who lived in a wood. He had a little wheelbarrow, and passed his time in a very moral and useful manner picking up slugs and snails. Yet there was something lacking in his life. The King of the world passed through that wood very early every morning, and made all things beautiful and new, but the brownie had never seen him. He longed to, but something prevented it. He had one cherished possession, a lovely little green blanket which had fallen out of the fairy queen's chariot and which he had not been able to help keeping for himself. It was very cold in the wood at night but the blanket kept him so warm and cosy that he never woke up to see the King of the world. And one day there came to him a shepherd who looked deep into the soul of the brownie and said to him: 'Haven't you seen the King of the world?' And the brownie said, 'No, I do so want to, but somehow I can't manage it.' Then the shepherd replied: 'But I seem to see something in your soul that keeps you from the vision; something that looks rather like a blanket.' And at that a terrible fight began in the heart of the brownie, a battle between wanting to go on being warm and comfortable in his blanket and longing to see the King of the world.

Perhaps . . . the ultimate choice which lies before us may turn out to be the brownie's choice between the heavenly vision and the blanket.

Evelyn Underhill, from a conference paper, *c.* April 1924

MARY WARD

In 1609 Mary Ward and her companions set up a school at St-Omer, near Calais, France. It was free to all classes, and over three years became very popular. The town suffered an outbreak of smallpox and Mary caught the disease. She was so ill that she was given the Last Sacraments. During her recovery she experienced something approaching a vision instructing her on her future foundation, which was to bring about a vast change: 'The Jesuits formed the first purely male society of bachelors. And with Mary Ward came the spinsters as an independent kind of religious order. But no, not with her, after her. She always intended herself and her followers as the feminine counterpart and complement to the S.J. – much against their will! – planning and pursuing this end with all the energy and vehemence of which she was capable.' (Ida Görres, Broken Lights, *London, 1964, pp. 180–1)*

The whole soul changed

About that time, in the year 1611, I fell sick in great extremity. Being somewhat recovered (by a vow made to send in pilgrimage to our Blessed Lady of Sichem), being alone, in some extraordinary repose of mind, I heard distinctly, not by sound of voice, but intellectually understood, these words: '*Take the same of the Society*'. So understood as that we were to take the same both in matter and manner, that only excepted which God by diversity of sex hath prohibited. These few words gave so great measure of light in that particular Institute, comfort and strength, and changed so the whole soul, as that it is impossible for me to doubt for that they came from him whose words are works.

Mother M. Salome, *Mary Ward: A Foundress of the 17th Century*, London, 1901, p. 77

Life's Journey and the Passage of the Soul

ꝯ

AGNES BEAUMONT

Agnes Beaumont of Edworth, Bedfordshire, a seventeenth-century Nonconformist under attack for her religious beliefs and practice by association with Bunyan, gives a moving account of her relationship with God just before and during her persecution. Her ability to reproduce her experiences in graphic imagery drawn from her surroundings, and in simple, direct statements, is exceptional.

Divine consolation

The Lord hath been pleased, since I was awakened, to exercise me with many and great trials; but, blessed be his gracious name, he hath caused all to work together for good to my poor soul, and hath often given me cause to say it was good for me that I have been afflicted. And oh, how great hath the kindness of God been to me in afflicting dispensations! In trials and temptations he never left me without his teaching and comforting presence, and I have often observed that, the more trouble and sorrow I have had either from within or without, the more of God's presence I have had; when I have been helped to keep close to him by prayer and supplication. And oh, how sweet is his presence when a poor soul is surrounded on every side with trouble! And for my part I have found trouble and sorrow, as David saith, none knoweth but God the sore trials and temptations that I have

47

warded through in my day, some outward, but more inward. But, on the other hand, none knows but God the sweet communion and consolation that it hath pleased a gracious God to give me in many of these hours of trouble. Oh, the great consolations and enlargements of heart, with fervent desires after Jesus Christ and His grace, which hath often made me thank God for trouble when I have found it drive me nearer to himself, to the throne of his grace. The Lord hath made troublesome times to me; praying times, humbling and mourning, and heart searching times. But one thing I have great cause to admire God's great goodness to me in, that before a trial hath come upon me I have had great consolations from God; insomuch that I have expected some thing to come upon me, and that [when] I had some trouble to meet that which hath often fallen out according to my thoughts, some times one scripture after another would run in my mind several days together. That would signify something I had to meet with, and that I must prepare for a trial, which would drive me into corners, to cry to the Lord to be with me. And oh, how hath the Lord as it were taken me up into the mount, that my soul hath been so raised and comforted as if it had been out of the body for a time. Many times in a day would the Lord lead me into his banqueting house, and his banner over me was love. . . .

About a quarter of a year before God was pleased to take my father, I had great and frequent enjoyments of God; and he was pleased to pour out a spirit of grace and supplication upon me in a wonderful manner, day and night, I may say. And, the Lord knowest it, there was scarce a corner in the house, or barns, or cow house, or stable, or closes, under the hedges, or in the wood, but I was made to pour out my soul to God. And some times before I have risen from my knees, I have been as if I had been in heaven, and as if my very heart would have break in pieces with joy and consolation, which hath caused floods of tears to fall from mine eyes with admiration of the love of Christ to such a great sinner as I was.

The Narrative of the Persecution of Agnes Beaumont: A Diary, ed. G. B. Harrison, London, n.d., pp. 3–7

EMILY DICKINSON

Emily Dickinson holds in delicate suspension our tragic feelings of powerlessness and suspicions of infinite possibility.

I saw no Way

I saw no Way – the Heavens were stitched –
I felt the Columns close –
The Earth reversed her Hemispheres –
I touch the Universe –

And back it slid – and I alone –
A Speck upon a Ball –
Went out upon Circumference –
Beyond the Dip of Bell –

Written *c.* 1862; Emily Dickinson, *Unpublished Poems*, Boston, 1935

MARGIAD EVANS

Margiad Evans wrote that if evil did indeed exist (and she inclined to accept it as a fact), she thought she could illustrate its beginnings and endings, while trying to bring illness unto death, age and decay into perspective.

Cobweb and chain

Supposing such a thing possible, you go out on an early autumn morning, the sun just risen, the light and shadows fresh, and a ghostly half substance, partly dew, partly cobweb stretching from stubble blade to stubble blade. You walk unhindered over the fields full of freedom and joy. This is youth. By the night time each impalpable silver thread is turned to iron chain – the fields and your feet are in fetters. This is age. . . . Repentance might break the chains, regret soften them. But I feel neither. I feel that I was deceived. Is this the lure? For Herbert writes that God lures us to His breast, and he if any man had insight into infinity. Why this ray of darkness on me while it is day? To teach me death? Compassion? That it has done and for that, if I have lived wrongly, to bring this disease, I would praise the disease, for to understand grief is beyond the understanding and the committing of art – even if a person's art is the only way he can think of God's self. There are two ways a person may live and be perfected. One is in his own spirit, the other in the necessities of others. I would put the latter lower, even now, for 'one thing only is necessary'.

Margiad Evans, *A Ray of Darkness*, London, 1952, p. 186

IDA GÖRRES

Ida Görres elicits the positive aspects of decay seen as development.

Growing old

I'm pondering a lot just now about the mysterious process of growing old – that stripping unto death. Yet I don't see it as something negative, not as descent into the dark valley, but rather as the climb to the last peak – before which one must rid oneself of all superfluous baggage, discarding all hampering equipment. The armour, the skins and wrappings the soul has laid upon itself for its own security would seem to be falling away, so that it must meet what is to come at last directly, naked.

Ida Friederike Görres, *Broken Lights*, tr. B. Waldstein-Wartenberg, London, 1964, p. 295

HADEWIJCH

For the 'mysticism of the essence' professed by Hadewijch, the ascent to God is a descent into his depths. She describes the soul's attempt to find the way of freedom, the road that must be taken to restore God's image in humankind, which has been distorted by sin. The way of return, she tells us, is the way of love which is simply total freedom, or self-stripping. All distinctive aspects of self disappear as the self divests itself of name, qualities and person, and loses itself in the simplicity of God's essence.

The way of freedom

For God, the soul is a free and open way, into which he can plunge from out of his furthest depths; and for the soul, in return, God is the way of freedom, towards the depths of the divine Being, which nothing can attain save the depths of the soul.

Hadewijch, Letter xviii, *Brieven*, 1, 73, Antwerp, 1947; see J. Leclercq et al., *The Spirituality of the Middle Ages*, London, 1968, p. 362

ST TERESA OF AVILA

The saint describes the distress that is bound up with our longing for divine consolation.

Holy desires

At other times there come upon me certain desires to serve God, with a vehemence so great that I cannot describe it, and accompanied with a certain pain at seeing how unprofitable I am. It seems to me then that there is nothing in the world, neither death nor martyrdom, that I could not easily endure. . . . I think I should like to raise my voice, and publish to all the world how important it is for men not to be satisfied with the common way. . . . These desires are such that I am melted away in myself, for I seem to desire what I cannot have. The body seems to me to hold me in prison, through its inability to serve God and my state in anything; for if it were not for the body, I might do very great things, so far as my strength would allow; and thus, because I see myself without any power whatever to serve God, I feel this pain in a way wholly indescribable; the issue is delight, recollection, and the consolation of God.

The Life of St Teresa of Avila by Herself, tr. David Lewis, London, 1962, p. 359

CHRISTINA ROSSETTI

Many of Christina Rossetti's poems were inspired by the Christian year and by acts of worship. They are devotional because liturgically based, but also because, under the influence of the Tractarian theologian John Keble, she treated poetry as primarily a means of seeking God, and the expression of profound religious longing as the most admirable of poetic aims. To convey a personal experience of nature in verse was a common aim of nineteenth-century poets; for Christina it meant reproducing an intense religious experience in a concentrated form. 'Up-hill' (written on 29 June 1858) is a poem of aspiration and consolation, which echoes such traditional forms as the ballad, and consolidates the yearnings of a woman who has experienced illness and disappointment in love.

Up-hill

Does the road wind up-hill all the way?
Yes, to the very end.
Will the day's journey take the whole long day?
From morn to night, my friend.

But is there for the night a resting-place?
A roof for when the slow dark hours begin.
May not the darkness hide it from my face?
You cannot miss that inn.

Shall I meet other wayfarers at night?
Those who have gone before.
Then must I knock, or call when just in sight?
They will not keep you standing at the door.

Shall I find comfort, travel-sore and weak?
Of labour you shall find the sum.
Will there be beds for me and all who seek?
Yea, beds for all who come.

Poetical Works of Christina Georgina Rossetti, ed. William Michael
Rossetti, London, 1935, p. 339

ST EDITH STEIN

*Edith Stein conceived of progress in the Christan life as becoming
ever more Christlike in the practice of 'cross-gender' virtues.*

Human perfection

Christ embodies the ideal of human perfection: in him all bias
and defects are removed, and the masculine and feminine virtues
are united and their weaknesses redeemed; therefore, his true followers will be progressively exalted over their natural limitations.
That is why we see in holy men a womanly tenderness and a truly
maternal solicitude for the souls entrusted to them while in holy
women there is manly boldness, proficiency, and determination.

Essays on Women, in *Collected Works of Edith Stein*, vol. II, p. 84; also
in Sarah Borden, *Edith Stein*, London, 2003, p. 72

EVELYN UNDERHILL

Evelyn Underhill was well aware that stale conventions were destructive and that innovation could be life-giving and, indeed, essential.

Christian revolution

The coming of the Kingdom is perpetual. Again and again freshness, novelty, power from beyond the world, break in by unexpected paths, bringing unexpected change. Those who cling to tradition and fear all novelty in God's relation with his world deny the creative activity of his Holy Spirit, and forget that what is now tradition was once innovation: that the real Christian is always a revolutionary, belongs to a new race, and has been given a new name and a new song.

M. Cropper, *Life of Evelyn Underhill*, London, 1958, p. 225

Autobiography and Personal Testament

⋇

ST CATHERINE OF GENOA

St Catherine of Genoa uses the familiar image of nourishment and elimination to describe the purgation or annihilation of inadequacies that begins in this life and continues after death if humans are to become the perfect beings that they are intended to be.

The chief end of humankind

As for the annihilating of mere existence, which has to occur in God, take bread, and eat it. When you have eaten it, its substance goes to nourish the body, and the rest is eliminated, because nature cannot use it at all, and indeed, if nature were to retain it, the body would die. Now, if that bread were to say to you: 'Why do you remove me from my being? if I could, I would defend myself to conserve myself, an action natural to every creature': you would answer: 'Bread, your being was ordained for a support for my body, a body which is of more worth than you; and therefore you ought to be more contented with your end than with your being. Live for your end, and you will not care about your being, but you will exclaim (to the body): "Swiftly, swiftly draw me forth from my being, and put me within the operation of that end of mine, for which I was created" . . .'

The soul, by the operation of God eliminates from the body all the superfluities and evil habits acquired by sin, and retains within itself the purified body, which body thenceforth performs its operations by means of these purified senses. . . . And, when the soul has consumed all the evil inclinations of the body, God consumes all the imperfections of the soul.

Friedrich von Hügel, *The Mystical Element of Religion as Studied in Saint Catherine of Genoa and Her Friends*, vol. I, London, 1908, p. 270

ELEANOR DAVIES

Eleanor Davies, who called her books and pamphlets her 'babes', was one of the most outspoken, if consistently bizarre, Puritan critics of the established Church and Laudian high-church practice in the reign of Charles I. Her works often have a biblical title, such as her 1648 The Writing on the wall, a warning to Charles I from Eleanor Davies, given to the Elector Prince Charles of the Rhine, or her 1625 A Warning to the Dragon and all his Angels. They were generally, as here, composed in a semi-colloquial choppy prose typical of ranters of the period and, at best, reminiscent of the Latin of Seneca.

Utterly undone

And before the great and dreadful day of the Lord's coming: when sent that prophet which for a sign of it, foreshowing with what plagues he will smite them, and truly never greater known, than at this very time: so take this into consideration, as probable as other things, before they came to pass; for mercy, and judgements going together, in these last days revealed . . . shall cancel that opinion of old, of hell to be a place or prison without redemption as it stands not in truth well with equity, where mercy is so immeasurable for the offence of our first deceived parents; who knew not what they did: that for their cause, so many without compassion, and commiseration, utterly should be undone and cast away, whereas SODOM for so few, their sakes had been spared when pressed, shall not the Judge of all the world do right?

Autobiography and Personal Testament

Eleanor Davies, *The Restitution of Reprobates*, London, 1644; in Diane Watt, *Secretaries of God: Women Prophets in Late Medieval and Early Modern England*, Cambridge, 1997, p. 143

HROSWITHA OF GANDERSHEIM

In the preface to her Gesta Ottonis, *a commissioned epic on the ruler, Hroswitha confesses (elegantly, and thereby demonstrating her literary ability) her inability as a woman writer to portray events and a world she cannot know in detail. The humility is genuine, yet permissibly ironic to the degree that it follows recognized convention.*

An appeal for guidance

I journeyed like one who, not knowing the route, is about to travel through a vast unknown ravine, where every path lies concealed, covered by thick snow; led on by no guide, only by signals of direction received beforehand, such a one would now stray onto by-paths, now unexpectedly hit the right path again, until at last, having reached the midpoint of the densely crowding trees, he would choose a spot for his longed-for rest, and there, staying his step, would dare to continue, until another came across him and could guide him, or he found a previous traveller's footprints he could follow. No otherwise did I, commanded to penetrate the vast region of glorious events, traverse the manifold paths of the royal deeds faltering and wavering, very ill at ease, and, utterly exhausted by them, sink to rest in silence in a suitable spot; nor do I undertake to climb the pinnacle of imperial excellence without guidance.

'Hroswitha', in Peter Dronke, *Women Writers of the Middle Ages*, Cambridge, 1984, p. 76

MARGARET FELL

Margaret Fell produced one of the best-argued and most cogent justifications by scriptural warranty of the right of women to speak and write on religious matters.

Women speaking in the Church

Whereas it hath been an objection in the minds of many, and several times hath been objected by the clergy, or ministers and others, against women's speaking in the Church; and so consequently may be taken, that they are condemned for meddling in the things of God: the ground of which objection is taken from the Apostle's words, which he wrote in his first Epistle to the Corinthians, Chap. 14. Vers. 34, 35. And also what he wrote to Timothy in the first Epistle, Chap. 2. Vers. 11, 12. But how far they wrong the Apostle's Intentions in these Scriptures, we shall show clearly. . . . But . . . God himself hath manifested his will and mind concerning women, and unto women . . . God hath put no such difference between the male and female, as men would make.

Let this word of the Lord, which was from the beginning, stop the mouths of all that oppose women's speaking in the power of the Lord; for he hath put enmity between the woman and the serpent; and if the seed of the woman speak not, the seed of the serpent speaks; for God hath put enmity between the two seeds; and it is manifest, that those that speak against the woman and her seed's speaking, speak out of the envy of the old serpent's seed. And God hath fulfilled his word and his promise. When the fulness of time was come, he sent forth his Son, made of a woman, made under the law, that we might receive the adoption of sons, Gal. 4. 4, 5.

Moreover, the Lord is pleased, when he mentions his Church, to call her by the name of woman, by his prophets, saying, I have called thee as a woman forsaken, and grieved in spirit, and as a wife of youth, Is. 54. Again, How long wilt thou go about, thou back-sliding daughter? For the Lord hath created a new thing in the earth, a woman shall compass a man, Jer. 31. 22. And David, when he was speaking of Christ and his Church, he saith, the King's daughter is all glorious within, her clothing is of wrought gold, she shall be brought unto the King; with gladness and rejoicing shall they be brought; they shall enter into the King's palace, Psal. 45. And also King Solomon in his song, where he speaks of Christ and his Church, where she is complaining and calling for Christ, he saith, if thou knowest not, O thou fairest among women, go thy way by the footsteps of the flock, Cant. 1. 8. c. 5. 9. And John, when he saw the wonder that was in heaven, he saw a woman clothed with the sun, and the moon under her feet, and upon her head a crown of twelve stars; and there appeared another wonder in heaven, a great red dragon stood ready to devour her Child. Here appears the envy of the dragon, Rev. 12.

Thus much may prove, that the Church of Christ is represented as a woman; and those that speak against this woman's speaking, speak against the Church of Christ, and the seed of the Woman, which seed is Christ; that is to say, those that speak against the power of the Lord, and the Spirit of the Lord speaking in a woman, simply by reason of her sex, or because she is a woman, not regarding the seed, and spirit, and power that speaks in her; such speak against Christ and his Church, and are of the seed of the serpent, wherein lodgeth enmity.

Margaret Fell, *Women's Speaking Justified, Proved, and Allowed of by the Scriptures, All Such as Speak by the Spirit and Power of the Lord Jesus. And How Women Were the First That Preached the Tidings of the Resurrection of Jesus, and Were Sent by Christ's Own Command, Before He Ascended to the Father*, London, n.d.

IDA GÖRRES

Ida Görres had an unrivalled ability to sum up acknowledged positives in an original and arresting way.

Monasticism and marriage

The Church, too, has her own bold Utopias: powerful, daring enough to make history, to change people: first, breath-taking in its audacity, monasticism: to live like the angels – fiery messengers of love and of truth – hovering above sex, possessions, power, struggle. The other, marriage: for ever indissoluble, an incomprehensible union of sex, Eros, friendship, love, Agape, fertility – all things which the Ancients assigned to diverse and often hostile gods: and in this and beyond it symbol, too, of the mystery of the 'oneing' of God and man, God and creation.

Ida Friederike Görres, *Broken Lights*, tr. B. Waldstein-Wartenberg, London, 1964, p. 143

JEANNE-MARIE BOUVIER DE LA MOTTE-GUYON

Madame Guyon gives a moving account of her childhood and negative relationship with her mother. In spite of her mother's lack of interest in her, Mme Guyon's unhappy experience enabled her to develop resilience and independence of mind at an early age. She knew that children should be brought up in a loving and harmonious atmosphere. She almost died at birth and was only two and a half when sent to an Ursuline convent. A little later, she was despatched to the Benedictines, where she was often sick and pleaded to be sent home.

On my return, my mother having a maid in whom she placed confidence, left me again to the care of servants. It is a great fault, of which mothers are guilty, when under pretext of external devotions, or other engagements, they suffer their daughters to be absent from them. I forbear not condemning that unjust partiality with which parents treat some of their children. It is frequently productive of divisions in families, and even the ruin of some. Impartiality, by uniting children's hearts together, lays the foundation of lasting harmony and unanimity.

I would I were able to convince parents, and all who have the care of youth, of the great attention they require, and how dangerous it is to let them be for any length of time from under their eye, or to suffer them to be without some kind of employment. This negligence is the ruin of multitudes of girls.

How greatly it is to be lamented, that mothers who are inclined to piety, should pervert even the means of salvation to their destruction and commit the greatest irregularities while apparently pursuing that which should produce the most regular and circumspect conduct.

Thus, because they experience certain gains in prayer, they would be all day long at church; meanwhile their children are running to destruction. We glorify God most when we prevent what may offend Him. What must be the nature of that sacrifice which is the occasion of sin! God should be served in His own way. Let the devotion of mothers be regulated so as to prevent their daughters from straying. Treat them as sisters, not as slaves. Appear pleased with their little amusements. The children will delight then in the presence of their mothers, instead of avoiding it. If they find so much happiness with them, they will not dream of seeking it elsewhere. Mothers frequently deny their children any liberties. Like birds constantly confined to a cage, they no sooner find means of escape than off they go, never to return. In order to render them tame and docile when young, they should be permitted sometimes to take wing, but as their flight is weak, and closely watched, it is easy to retake them when they escape. Little flight gives them the habit of naturally returning to their cage which becomes an agreeable confinement. I believe young girls should be treated in a manner something similar to this. Mothers should indulge them in an innocent liberty, but should never lose sight of them.

To guard the tender minds of children from what is wrong, much care should be taken to employ them in agreeable and useful matters. They should not be loaded with food they cannot relish. Milk suited to babies should be administered to them not strong meat which may so disgust them, that when they arrive at an age when it would be proper nourishment, they will not so much as taste it. Every day they should be obliged to read a little in some good book, spend some time in prayer, which must be suited rather to stir the affections, than for meditation. Oh, were this method of education pursued, how speedily would many irregularities cease! These daughters becoming mothers, would educate their children as they themselves had been educated.

Parents should also avoid showing the smallest partiality in the treatment of their children. It begets a secret jealousy and hatred among them, which frequently augments with time, and even continues until death. How often do we see some children the idols of the house, behaving like absolute tyrants, treating their brothers and sisters as so many slaves according to the example of father and mother. And it happens many times, that the favourite proves a scourge to the parents while the poor despised and hated one becomes their consolation and support.

My mother was very defective in the education of her children. She suffered me whole days from her presence in company with the servants, whose conversation and example were particularly hurtful to one of my disposition. My mother's heart seemed wholly centred in my brother. I was scarcely ever favoured with the smallest instance of her tenderness or affection. I therefore voluntarily absented myself from her. It is true, my brother was more amiable than I but the excess of her fondness for him, made her blind even to my outward good qualities. It served only to discover my faults, which would have been trifling had proper care been taken of me.

Mme Guyon, *Autobiography*, tr. T. T. Allen, London, 1897, Vol. I, ch. 2

LUCY HUTCHINSON

Lucy Hutchinson had a rigorous scholarly conscience and was constantly concerned to reflect the 'original of things': the divine order that governed the universe, made sure that the world mirrored heaven, and made it possible for humankind ('Adam') to reflect the image of the Creator already enshrined in the human constitution. Similarly, conscientious humans under the guidance of Scripture and divine inspiration were bound to ensure that society, as in the governance of the realm of England, should perfectly conform to the union between God and humanity already established in mystical form. This demanded continual devout inquiry, even at an early age.

Knowledge of God

It pleased God that, through the good instructions of my mother, and the sermons she carried me to, I was convinced that the knowledge of God was the most excellent study, and accordingly applied myself to it, and to practise as I was taught. I used to exhort my mother's maids much, and to turn their idle discourses to good subjects; but I thought when I had done this on the Lord's Day, and every day performed my due tasks of reading and praying that then I was free to do anything that was not sin; for I was not at that time convinced of the vanity of conversation which was not scandalously wicked. I thought it no sin to learn or hear witty songs and amorous sonnets or poems. . . .

Lucy Hutchinson, *Memoirs of Colonel Hutchinson*, London, 1908, p. viii

CORRIE TEN BOOM

Corrie ten Boom describes the extraordinary conversion (which became complete after the war) of a Dutch collaborator in the prison where she and her sister were gaoled for protecting and hiding Jews from the Germans and Dutch Fascists and collaborators during the occupation of the Netherlands.

The work of Christ

Hans Rahms was a caseworker in Scheveningen prison during Betsie's [her sister] and my interrogations . . . while we were in prison the Lord touched Mr Rahm's heart so that Betsie and I were both able to tell him about Jesus and his love. Later, in camp at Vught, Betsie told me that she had been able to say, 'Mr Rahms, it is important to talk about Jesus but it is more important to talk with him. Would you mind if I prayed with you?' Five times she was ordered to report to this man for interrogation and five times she prayed with him – she, the prisoner and he, her judge. Through this, Hans Rahms became a friend instead of an enemy and we were recipients of his help several times during our imprisonment.

One morning, just before a hearing, he showed some papers to me. When I saw them, I knew that many lives were in great danger, for the papers contained detailed information about my underground activities. I could see on them the names of friends, Jews, and underground workers. When he asked me to explain the papers, I could not. The silence that followed was one of the most agonizing moments of my life. Then, suddenly, that moment was transformed into joy, for the judge took all the papers, opened the stove door, and threw them into the fire! Before my eyes, I saw the flames destroying every name and at that instant, I understood the verse, Colossians 2:14, 'Blotting out the handwriting of ordinances that was against us, which was contrary to us, and took it out of the way, nailing it to his cross'.

That is what Christ did for us, and for me. . . .

Corrie ten Boom, *Prison Letters*, London, 1975, pp. 93–4

Autobiography and Personal Testament

EVELYN UNDERHILL

In her own particular world of spiritual counselling and her thinking about the importance of ecumenism, Evelyn Underhill was moving towards a position not wholly unlike that reached by Dietrich Bonhoeffer under the much more radical and dire situation of Christianity in Nazi Germany. She did not go so far as to recommend 'religionless Christianity' or learning to 'live in the world as though there were no God', but the stance she proposes here is close to Bonhoeffer's 'secular holiness' and his proposals for the renewal of church structure and attitudes.

The spirit of exploration

In the days that are coming, I am sure that Christianity will have to move out from the churches and chapels, or rather spread out far beyond the devotional focus of its life, and justify itself as a complete philosophy of existence, beautifying and enriching all levels of being, physical, social and mental as well as spiritual, telling the truth about God and man, and casting its transfiguring radiance on the whole of that world in which man has to live. It must in fact have the courage to apply its own inherent sacramentation, without limitation, to the whole mixed experience of humanity, and in the light of this interpretation show men the way out of their confusions, miseries, and sins. Only those who have learned to look at the eternal with the disinterested loving gaze, the objective unpossessive delight of worship, who do see the stuff of common life with the light shining through it, will be able to do that.

The spirit of worship is the very spirit of exploration. It has never finished discovering and adoring the ever new perfections of that which it loves. 'My beloved is like strange islands!' said St John of the Cross, in one of his great poems. Islands in an uncharted ocean, found by the intrepid navigators after a long and difficult voyage, which has made great demands on faith, courage, and perseverance; islands that reveal beauties that we had never dreamed of and a life of independent loveliness, to which our dim everyday existence gives no clue; yet never reveal everything, always have some unanswered questions, keep their ultimate secret still.

M. Cropper, *Life of Evelyn Underhill*, London, 1958, pp. 204–5

SIMONE WEIL

Simone Weil believed that 'Everything without exception which is of value in me comes from somewhere other than myself, not as a gift but as a loan which must be ceaselessly renewed.' In a letter of 1942 to Gustave Thibon, who protected her from Nazi persecution for her Jewish ancestry, she renounces ownership of her writings, but also egotism.

Submission

I hope that Destiny will spare the house at Saint Marcel – the house inhabited by three beings who love each other. That is something very precious. Human existence is so fragile a thing and exposed to such dangers that I cannot love without trembling. I have never yet been able to resign myself to the fact that all human beings except myself are not completely preserved from every possibility of harm. That shows a serious falling short in the duty of submission to God's will. . . .

I only regret not being able to confide to you all that I still bear undeveloped within me. Luckily, however, what is within me is either valueless or else it exists outside me in a perfect form, in a place of purity where no harm can come to it and whence it will always be able to come down again That being so, nothing concerning me can have any kind of importance.

I also like to think that after the slight shock of separation you will not feel any sorrow about whatever may be in store for me, and that if you sometimes happen to think of me you will do so as one thinks of a book one read in childhood. I do not want ever to occupy a different place from that in the hearts of those I love, because then I can be sure of never causing them any unhappiness. . . .

Simone Weil, *Gravity and Grace*, London, 1952; also in J. Cumming, ed., *Letters from Saints to Sinners*, London and New York, 1996, pp. 119–20

Direction and Counselling

꩜

ST BERNADETTE OF LOURDES

As a Sister of Notre Dame at Nevers, Bernadette was able to escape disturbing publicity and continual questioning about her intense experiences, and develop her own devotional and spiritual life without hindrance. She never forgot her brothers and sister. Her written advice shows the same clarity and immediacy as her initial accounts of her visions.

Sound advice

1 July 1876
To her brother
My dear Jean-Marie,

In her letter our cousin Nicholau tells me that you will probably be discharged from the army this year. Let me know what you are going to do. I am sure that you realize, although I live at such a distance, that I am as interested in all you do as if I were on the spot. Rest assured that I do not ask any questions out of idle curiosity. Since our dear father and mother are dead it is my duty as the eldest sister to watch over you.

I must say that just now I am very anxious about your future and Pierre's. Every day I pray that our Lord and our blessed Lady will guide you. Above all, I firmly advise you to remember your Christian duty. Then you will take strength in all your troubles and problems. I know that soldiers have a lot to put up with,

and have to do so without protest. If when they got up they were
to say to our Lord every morning this short sentence: 'My God,
I wish to do and to endure everything today for love of you,' they
would store up immeasurable treasure in heaven! If a soldier did
that and performed his Christian duties as faithfully as possible,
he would earn the same reward as any monk in a cloister!

Your sister,

Bernadette

J. Cumming, ed., *Letters from Saints to Sinners*, London and New York,
1996, p. 57

SAINT BRIDGET OF SWEDEN

Ida Görres remarked that in St Bridget's Revelations *(a formid-
able volume of at least 700 double-columned pages when printed
in 1664, and very taken up with purgatory), the judgement scenes
show people standing between their good and bad angels. The
Devil is a prosecutor who records our sins but cannot see our
good thoughts, which are in the good angel's book. In his 'great
indictment' against a good person, the 'Devil's pièce de résistance
is not his misdeeds, but rather the good left undone (what people
these days fondly think they've discovered – as against "crude"
medieval morality!). And please note, even in a man's virtues and
good works the Devil stresses the lack of supernatural motives,
of pure love of God and zeal for his honour. God himself, of
course, draws the final balance. Bridget's revelations were so
controversial in the early Middle Ages that their extreme nature
was discussed in detail at the Council of Constance. Nevertheless,
much of her advice was quite straightforward and remains help-
ful, as in her warnings about over-confidence and the need for
vigilance in the religious life.*

Pride comes before a fall

We learn from Scripture that Jacob laboured as a servant for the sake of Rachel and that his overwhelming love made time seem to pass like lightning, because his affection for her took all the hardship from his labours. But Jacob was foiled precisely when he thought that his wishes were granted. Yet he did not stop working, because true love does not reckon the cost until it achieves its object. As in ordinary life, so it is in matters spiritual. In order to acquire heavenly rewards, many people work very hard at praying and doing pious works, but just when they imagine that they have reached the state of contemplative peace, they are assailed by temptations. Their problems grow, and at the very point when they think they are almost perfect, they discover that they are quite imperfect. This is not surprising, since temptations are sent to try us, but also to perfect us.

Some people find that they are tempted more when they are first converted to the spiritual life. They grow much stronger eventually. Others are more seriously tempted in the middle and at the end of their lives, and people like that have to watch their conduct with great care, never take their strength of character for granted, and work all the more assiduously. . . . You should not be astonished if temptations increase even when you are old. As long as you are allowed to live, you are liable to be tempted. On the other hand, temptation is an opportunity to seek perfection and never become presumptuous.

Bridget of Sweden, *Revelationes Extravagantes*, pt. V, ed. L. Hollmann, Uppsala, 1956, cols 121–2

ST JANE FRANCES DE CHANTAL

St Jeanne de Chantal was a very proficient founder and governor of the eighty-six religious houses she administered, and much in demand as a religious and moral counsellor of women of high social station. She did not hesitate to extend her advice to her own daughter, Françon, to whom she wrote on 13 April 1620.

Jeanne's husband had died in a hunting accident, and she had to ensure that her dedication to the religious life did not lead her to neglect the control over a child's choice of spouse that morality and convention required at that time.

Preparing for marriage

May God be blessed for having guided you so wisely and fortunately as you prepare for your marriage. May his divine goodness guarantee you perfect peace. My darling girl, as things progress I am all the happier. Monsieur de Toulonjon is, I am convinced, the kindest of men. He has returned as pleased as possible and there is every reason for us to feel the same way. Dear Françon, your trust has delighted me greatly, but for my part God knows how I have prayed and wished to see you settled happily. He knows how much more profoundly I have felt your problem than my own. Your contentment is always my main concern; never doubt that. Rest assured that my love for you carried me away on this occasion, because I saw that it was the best for you. We certainly owe all this to the goodness of our Lord, who has cared for you and for me and has heard our prayers. The enclosed letter will tell you how much his lordship of Bourges also wants this marriage to take place.

Stay firm and if anxieties about this or that cross your mind, shut them out and do not let them in again on any account. Follow reason in everything as well as my own everyday advice. Believe me, my dear child, it is very good for you; if you carry on heeding it, you will find how wise it is. Do not forget your promise to write out at length all you think and feel, and to let me know if God has joined your heart to that of Monsieur de Toulonjon. Above all, I hope and wish that to be so, and I trust that God will have blessed our first meeting accordingly. As for me, darling, I can only repeat what I have already told you most sincerely: I wholeheartedly approve of him. The affection I have for him is warmer than I can express. Indeed, none of our friends and relatives who know him could be more satisfied with him than you and I.

Monsieur de Toulonjon is very anxious about your rings. He wants to send me a large selection of all the precious stones in Paris, so that I can buy whatever I choose for you. Actually, I should prefer you to take none of them. Frankly, my dear, ladies of quality no longer wear jewellery at Court. That is left to the wives of the townsfolk. But you must make your own decision when you come here. However, I do not know how I can persuade Monsieur de Toulonjon to share my opinion, for he has begged me, just for a start, to send you pearls and earrings and a vanity bag full of diamonds, which is all that ladies now carry with their gowns. But we really must not let him have his own way in such extravagance. He so much wants to please you that he will go to any lengths to give you whatever you want. If ever a wife ought to be quite happy, it is you. But you must realize how discreet you have to be in trying to restrain him. It would be best to be rather economical and to spend your money on useful things rather than on fripperies and show. I really do not want my Françon to go in for that sort of thing. Anyway, my own reputation is at stake, for you are my daughter and therefore you should be discreet and careful and arrange your life appropriately and profitably.

Finally, you should wear a wedding-dress. I do not want any ostentation in your marriage. I mean that absolutely. Monsieur de Toulonjon told me that you did not wish to be married during May. Doesn't your conscience worry you in this regard? It is rank superstition. On the other hand, however much he wants it, I do not think May will be possible.

The more I see of him the more I like him. The more, too, I realize that we should thank God for your happy engagement. Send him a very polite and warm letter. Be quite frank and open with him and show that you return his love. In future there is no need to stand on ceremony with him. His servant is downstairs waiting for my letter. My sole desire, dearest Françon, is that you should love your future husband with your whole heart. Good-bye, my dearest. Be quite frank when you write to me.

J. Cumming, ed., *Letters From Saints to Sinners*, London and New York, 1996, pp. 149–51

DHUODA

Dhuoda reminds her son of her concern for him and of his own duty towards his brother, who was taken from her when only some months old.

Hold up your heart

I, Dhuoda, am always with you to encourage you. In the future, should I fail you by my absence, you have this little moral work as a reminder, so that as you read in spirit and body and as you pray to God you may be able to look upon me as if in a mirror. Then you may clearly see your duty to me. My son, my firstborn son – you will have other teachers to present you with works of fuller and richer usefulness, but not anyone like me, your mother, whose heart burns on your behalf.

Read the words I address to you, understand them and fulfill them in action. And when your little brother, whose name I still do not know, has received the grace of baptism in Christ, do not hesitate to teach him, to educate him, to love him, and to call him to progress from good to better. When the time has come that he has learned to speak and read, show him this little volume gathered together into a handbook by me and written down in your name. Urge him to read it, for he is your flesh and your brother. I, your mother Dhuoda, urge you, as if I even now spoke to both of you, that you 'Hold up your heart' from time to time when you are oppressed by troubles of this world, and 'Look upon him who reigns in heaven' and is called God.

Dhuoda, *Handbook for William: A Carolingian Woman's Counsel for Her Son*, tr. Carol Neel, Washington, DC, 1991, p. 13

ANN GRIFFITHS

Saunders Lewis, a poet and playwright of international stature able to place Ann Griffiths appropriately in the great European mystical and literary traditions, wrote that the 'assurance of the sublime holiness and infinity of God is the key to all the poetry of Ann Griffiths . . . the word which comes most frequently in her poetry, the word which reveals her response, is rhyfeddu *(to wonder), and the adjective* rhyfedd *(wonderful) and the noun* rhyfeddod *. . . to worship the plan of salvation (without anything of self or any thought of self coming into it) . . . to look upon it together with the angels and worship it for its own sake, on account of its holiness and its divinity – it is for this that Ann Griffiths yearns' ('Ann Griffiths: a literary survey', in James Coutts, ed.,* Homage to Ann Griffiths, *Penarth, 1976, pp. 20–3). An account of a visit to Ann by the great Calvinistic Methodist scholar Thomas Charles tells us that he came away speechless with fear and excitement after meeting what she called her 'grieving soul . . . leaping into joy'. One of Ann's letters to friends reveals some part of her intense experience of the sovereignty of God that so impressed her contemporaries.*

A letter about the Holy Spirit

My dear Sister, the thing I'm most concerned about just now has to do with offending the Holy Spirit. I have been thinking of that passage of Scripture which says that we should always remember that our bodies are temples of the Holy Spirit living within us. I must admit that even the scant attention I have now given to due consideration of the wonders of the Spirit, and how he lives or resides in a believing person, persuades me that until now I have never been genuinely concerned about grieving him. I have been able to grasp one reason, which is also the main one, why what is actually a serious offence made so little impression on me, and that is because I conceived of so infinitely great a Person in terms that were, yes, quite crude and, indeed, blasphemous. . . .

I thought about the Persons of the Blessed Trinity in the following way. Now I feel most ashamed that I could ever have done so, but I have to tell someone, because this kind of approach is harmful. I thought of the Father and of the Son as co-equal Persons, but saw the Person of the Holy Spirit as a functional being subordinate to Father and Son. That was an utterly incorrect image of a Person who has to be divine, omnipresent, omniscient and all-powerful in order to continue and complete the good work he has started in connection with the free covenant and wisdom of the Trinity with regard to those creatures who are the objects of the three Persons' primordial love. I hope that I can share the privilege of being such an individual.

Dear sister, I am thirsty to increase the intensity of my belief in the personal presence of the Holy Spirit in my life, and to do so by means of revelation and not of imagination, as if I thought I could understand exactly how or by what means he is present, for speculation is plain idolatry. . . .

My dear sister, I long (and now think it more important than ever before) to spend the rest of my life devoting myself entirely, body and soul, to the time . . . when I shall depart from the tabernacle of this life. Dear sister, sometimes the thought of leaving this world is especially sweet. Of course, I am not happy about death itself, but about the immense achievement that results from it. It means saying goodbye to everything that is contrary to what God wants, and abandoning any possibility of disobeying God's law. Then strength will overcome all weakness, and we shall conform entirely to the law already inscribed in our hearts, and enjoy the vision of God for ever. At times, my dear sister, these matters fill my mind to such an extent that I neglect my earthly duties, and merely await the time of my dissolution, when I shall be with Christ for ever. Yet it is very good to see him here if only through a screen, when, sometimes, the Lord reveals through a glass darkly as much of his glory as my impoverished faculties can bear. . . .

From the letter to Elizabeth Evans in the National Library of Wales. Translated by John Griffiths.

HILDEGARD OF BINGEN

An abbot who was immensely depressed wrote to Hildegard to ask for advice. Her reply drew on her visions, and her knowledge of gardens and agriculture.

Drench your thoughts in the streams of scripture and study the example of the saints, then try to live like them. Do all this modestly and let the blossom flourish in your brothers like leaves and flowers on a tree. Be like the sun with your teaching, like the moon in your readiness to adapt, like the wind by your unwavering guidance, like gentle breezes in your forbearance, and like fire in the arousing and inspiring force of your instruction. Everything should begin with the first gleam of early dawn and end in blazing light.

Patrologia Latina 289A, Vol. 197, tr. J. Cumming, Paris, 1882

Like St Catherine of Siena, Hildegard did not hesitate to tell kings, popes and bishops how to behave, as when she wrote to King Conrad III.

Take a long, hard look at the giddy and fickle times you are living in. They are . . . moving inevitably towards injustice of so extreme and wanton a kind that even the justice of the Lord's own vineyards is threatened with destruction. We have entered a truly calamitous age when God's own precincts begin to reek with the acrid smoke of sorrow and affliction. Not only are the riches of the Church squandered, but the sacred estate itself is mauled as if by a pack of wolves and driven from its own home and mother country. What will all this lead to? To a vast number of people being forced into harsh solitude, to eke out their days serving God in poverty, profound remorse, and deep humiliation. And there is more to come. The mood of these times is degrading enough, but there are yet others on the horizon that menace us with their own brand of misery and wrongdoing.

Direction and Counselling

Hildegard wrote to Pope Anastasius IV (who reigned from 12 July 1153 to 3 December 1154) with the unswerving prophetic assurance drawn from her extraordinary visions:

The entire earth is confused and out of joint under the pressure of a constant flood of false ideas and doctrines, because human beings love what God has already condemned. And you, Rome, are just lying there like someone waiting to die. Can't you see that all the strength of the feet you have stood on so firmly for so long is being sapped and that they will soon give way under you? The trouble is that you have no burning love of justice but approve of it implicitly – in your sleep, that is! Your sheer numbness allows justice to slip away unnoticed. . . . The eye steals, the nose snuffs up and snuffs out, and the mouth kills, whereas healing and salvation come from the heart. The unparalleled light of a new dawn, new desire and new enthusiasm depend on the saving work of the heart. . . .

You just have to realize, man, that your powers of perception have grown weak and that you are too worn-out to curb the arrogant boastful behaviour of those in your charge! Why don't you stop these destructive men? Why not pull up these evil roots? Why are you so indifferent to Justice, your 'Heavenly Bride' and the King's own Daughter? Justice is ravished by the immorality of people howling like dogs, and squawking as inanely as chickens in the middle of the night. . . . Why do you permit these people to lead such licentious lives? Can't you see that they are just staggering around in the darkness of their own stupidity, no better than hens that screech out at night, alerting the robbers to their prey and making their own fate inevitable?

Hildegard von Bingen, *Briefwechsel*, Salzburg, 1965, pp. 39–40

KATHERINE PARR

A manuscript prayer of characteristic simplicity, which stresses the need for patience, due consideration, and the practice of humane virtues under divine guidance, appears on the flyleaf of Katherine's prayer book, still in existence.

Katherine's creed

Delight not in the multitude of ungodly men,
and have no pleasure in them,
for they fear not God.

Trust not in wicked wretches,
for they shall not help in the day of punishment and wrath.

Be gentle to hear the work of God,
That you may understand it,
And make a true answer with wisdom.

Be swift to hear and slow in giving answer.

Be not a privy accuser as long as you live,
And use no slander with your tongue.

See that you justify small and great alike.

Refuse not the prayer of one that is in trouble,
And turn not away your face from the needy.

Katherine Parr, ms prayer from a volume in the Dent-Brocklehurst collection at Sudeley Castle, Gloucestershire

ST TERESA OF AVILA

Teresa tells us that she feared a 'discontented nun more than I fear many devils'. She was keen to correct gossiping, over-sensitiveness, affected or childish behaviour, and any departure from the good, honest, 'ordinary' virtues that she admired in her nuns. Ribera says that Teresa herself was so far from caring for honours that 'not only did she wish to leave Avila because she was held there in high esteem, and retire with her dowry to another house of the Order far away where she would be unknown, but she also wanted to become a lay sister so as to do the meanest and hardest work', and would have done so 'if she not been prevented by authority'.

True honour

Oh, God help me, sisters! Would that we realized in what true honour consists and how it is forfeited! I am not speaking about what we are at the present moment: it would indeed be shameful if we did not recognize this. I apply it to myself in the days when I prided myself on my honour, as is the custom of the world, without knowing what the word really meant. Oh! how ashamed I feel at recalling what used to annoy me then, although I was not a person accustomed to stand on ceremony. Still, I did not realize where the essential point of honour lay, for I neither knew nor cared for real honour, which is of some profit because it benefits the soul.

How truly has someone said: 'Honour and profit do not go together!' I do not know whether he applied this meaning to it, still, quoting his words as they stand, the soul's profit and what men call honour can never go together. The world's antagonism to this is most astounding. Thank God for taking us out of it! (May he always keep its spirit as far from this house as it is now! Heaven defend us from monasteries, where the inmates are sensitive as to their fancied rights: they will never pay much honour to God there. What can be more absurd than for religious to stand upon their dignity on such petty points that I am absolutely surprised at them! You know nothing about such things, sisters: I will tell you so that you may be on your guard.)

The devil has not forgotten us – he has invented his honours in religious houses – he has settled the laws by which the dwellers rise and fall in dignity (as men do in the world), and they are jealous of their honour in surprisingly petty matters. Learned men must observe a certain order in their studies which I cannot understand: he who has read theology must not descend to read philosophy. This is a point of honour which consists in advancing and in not retrograding. If obedience obliged anyone to do the contrary, he would secretly take it as an affront and would find many who would take his part and say he had been ill-used. The devil would easily bring reasons even from the law of God by which to prove this. Even among nuns she who has been prioress must never fill any lower office: deference must be shown to the first in rank – there is no fear she will forget it; this even seems a merit for the Rule enjoins it. The thing is enough to make one laugh – or with better cause, to weep. Yes, for the Rule does not forbid me to be humble; this regulation I made to maintain order, but I ought not to be so strict about my dignity as to insist upon this point's being observed so exactly as the rest which perhaps I obey very slackly, while I will not overlook one jot or tittle of this one. Our perfection does not consist wholly in keeping this point of the Rule. Let others care for what concerns my rank and let me ignore it. The fact is that we are bent on rising higher, though we shall never rise to heaven by this path, and we will not think of descending.

St Teresa of Avila, *The Way of Perfection*, tr. A Benedictine of Stanbrook, rev. B. Zimmerman OCD, London, 1961, pp. 196–8

EVELYN UNDERHILL

In one of her lectures, Evelyn Underhill cited Angela of Foligno (a follower of St Francis) when talking of the importance of a lack of presumption and the always unfathomed mystery of God.

Make yourselves small

When she knew that she was dying, Angela called all her spiritual children to her, and blessed them all and said to them: 'Make yourselves small! Make yourselves small!' And after that she lay very still, and they heard her murmuring, 'No creature is sufficient! No intelligence, even of angels or of archangels is sufficient!' Those who were round her asked, 'What is it, Mother, for which the intelligence of angels and archangels is not sufficient?' And she said, 'To understand'.

Evelyn Underhill, *Mixed Pasture*, London, 1933, p. 39

MARY WARD

The final emphasis of Mary Ward's remarkable instructions to her forward-looking community on how its members should conduct themselves towards God, towards our neighbour, and towards themselves was on the need to be cheerful above all things.

Religious conduct

It very ill becomes a religious person to be faint-hearted, for she knows well that God is omnipotent, who can turn all to her profit, and that he loves her infinitely, and, therefore, will permit nothing which could hurt.

The true children of this company shall accustom themselves to act not out of fear, but solely from love, because they are called by God to a vocation of love.

A troubled dejected spirit will never love God perfectly, nor do much good to his honour.

Whoever would work much good in this congregation must have an entire mistrust in herself and great confidence in God. Prize thy honour higher than thy life, but esteem it little to lose both for the love of Jesus Christ.

We ought to work and suffer for God, and for the rest let him make use of us according to his good pleasure, for the fulfilment of his most holy will should be our sole wish and only desire.

Desire not the least thing which is contrary to God and thy conscience under the pretext and in the hope of attaining a great good.

Be ashamed to say that anything appears hard to thee in the service of God, for to those who love all is light.

Satisfy thyself with nothing which is less than God.

Divine love is like fire, which will not let itself be shut up, for it is impossible to love God and not to labour to extend his honour.

Show thyself at all time glad and joyful, for Almighty God loves a cheerful giver.

Mistrust in God ties as it were his hands, so that he cannot bestow upon us his blessing and his divine gifts.

Care not for what concerns thine own person, but stand up zealously for whatever touches God and his honour.

Prize thy calling highly and love it above all others, since the eternal truth has said in the Gospel, that he who keeps and teaches the commandments shall be great in the kingdom of heaven.

Whoever will serve God according to her state in this Institute must of necessity love the Cross, and be ready to suffer much for Christ's sake.

Be all things to all men, so that thou mayest win all for God, and be careful as much as thou canst to satisfy all.

Make use of gentle and kind words when thou reprovest any one, for thou wilt thus effect more than through those which are harsh and overbearing.

Love all men, but love them not on thine own account, but for God.

Ours shall most diligently be on their guard that they never speak of the defects of other people, and especially not of those of religious. They shall also not complain of one another, but preserve charity indissolubly as the peculiar virtue of our company.

Do not easily be offended at the doings of others, since thou canst not know what is their intention; but accustom thyself to put a good construction on all thou seest and hearest.

Although the conversion of souls is very pleasing to God, yet he loves the perfection of each one so greatly, that he wills not that any one should commit even the smallest sin, were the whole world to be converted thereby.

Take away from no one what he loves, unless thou givest him instead something he loves still better.

It is a greater grace to help to save souls than oneself to suffer martyrdom.

Do good and do it well.

Wherever thou findest thyself, remember that not the place, but the practices sanctify.

Whatever falls to thee to do, that perform as much as thou canst faithfully and diligently; but be not too careful as to how it may turn out, nor whether it will be hazardous or not, but commit it to the good God.

Let nothing disturb the peace of thy heart, not even thy sins.

As a thirsty man eagerly swallows whatever he receives to drink, so a thirster after perfection drinks in with joy every admonition, be it sweet or bitter.

In our calling, a cheerful mind, a good understanding, and a great desire after virtue are necessary, but of all three a cheerful mind is the most so.

Mother M. Salome, *Mary Ward: A Foundress of the 17th Century*, London, 1901, pp. 109–11

Faith and Renewal

꿔

ANNE ASKEW

The simple ballad in which Anne Askew states her staunch Christian faith was for many years as popular as such Nonconformist hymns of later periods of persecution as Bunyan's 'To be a pilgrim'.

A ballad which Anne Askew wrote and sang in Newgate gaol

Like as the armed knight
Appointed to the field,
With this world will I fight
And Faith shall be my shield.

Faith is that weapon strong
Which will not fail at need.
My foes, therefore, among
Therewith will I proceed.

As it is had in strength
And force of Christes way
It will prevail at length
Though all the devils say nay.

Faith in the fathers old
Obtained righteousness
Which make me very bold
To fear no world's distress.

I now rejoice in heart
And Hope bid me do so
For Christ will take my part
And ease me of my woe.

Thou sayest, Lord, who so knock,
To them wilt thou attend.
Undo, therefore, the lock
And thy strong power send.

More enemies now I have
Than hairs upon my head.
Let them not me deprave
But fight thou in my stead.

On thee my care I cast.
For all their cruel spite
I set not by their haste
For thou art my delight.

I am not she that list
My anchor to let fall
For every drizzling mist
My ship substantial.

Not oft use I to write
In prose nor yet in rhyme,
Yet will I show one sight
That I saw in my time.

I saw a royal throne
Where Justice should have sit
But in her stead was one
Of moody cruel wit.

Absorbed was righteousness
As of the raging flood
Satan in his excess
Sucked up the guiltless blood.

Then thought I, Jesus Lord,
When thou shalt judge us all
Hard is it to record
On these men what will fall.

Yet Lord, I thee desire
For that they do to me
Let them not taste the hire
Of their iniquity.

The Account of the Sufferings of Anne Askew . . . written by herself,
London, 1849, p. 98

ST CATHERINE OF GENOA

*We are told of St Catherine of Genoa that, on 11 November
1509, she was affected by an 'insupportable fire of infinite love'
when she was shown a single spark of pure love for a moment.
It was so forceful that, if it had lasted even a little longer, she
would have died. She could hardly eat or speak because of the
'penetrating wound of love that she had received in her heart',
but managed to describe the suffering she was sure must end in
perfect joy when the soul drawn by love of God has endured not
only this life, but purgatory. Nevertheless, she was aware that all
spiritual insights, including her own, are only approximations,
and possibly misleading. For instance, as Ida Görres pointed out,
Catherine of Genoa, though cited as the recognized witness to the
nature of purgatory, never had a vision of it, for her statements
are analogies, based on her own spiritual 'experiences of suffering and bliss: "So that's what it must be like in purgatory!"'*

Lost in her own self

This creature, all lost in her own self, found her true self in one instant in God. Although she reputed herself to be very poor, yet she remained rich in the divine love. She, knowing the grace and operation to be all from God, remained lost in herself, and living only in God. She gave her free-will to God, and God thereupon worked with its means. O the great wonder, to see human beings established in the midst of so many miseries, and yet God having so great a care of them! All tongues are incapable of expressing it, all intellects of understanding it. That person becomes foolish in the eyes of the world, to whom you, O Lord God, manifest even the slightest spark of your indescribable Love. You, O God, wish to exalt humans, and to make them as though they would have to die of a great martyrdom. . . .

I would not that as much as one single meritorious act be ascribed to my separate self, not even if it should convince me that I would never fall again and that my salvation would be certain as soon as I had accomplished it: for such an imputation would be for me as though from hell. I would rather remain in peril of eternal damnation than be saved by such an act of my separate being, and furthermore to be aware of it. . . .

So long as human beings are still capable of speaking of divine things, can savour them, understanding, remembering and desiring them, then they have not yet reached the harbour. . . . Should any human beings think they truly behold spiritual things as they really are, let them pluck out the eye of their presumption.

Friedrich von Hügel, *The Mystical Element of Religion as Studied in Saint Catherine of Genoa and Her Friends*, vol. I, London, 1908, pp. 188 ff.

EMILY DICKINSON

Emily Dickinson's poem perfectly states the lack of assurance that authentic conviction must accept.

Faith

Faith – is the Pierless Bridge
Supporting what We see
Unto the Scene that We do not –
Too slender for the eye

It bears the Soul as bold
As it were rocked in Steel
With Arms of Steel at either side –
It joins – behind the Veil

To what, could We presume
The Bridge would cease to be
To Our far, vacillating Feet
A first Necessity.

Written *c.* 1864; Emily Dickinson, *Further Poems*, Boston, 1929

MARY BAKER EDDY

Mrs Eddy believed that God is all in all and divine Mind, and that faith enables us to appreciate our condition as the idea and image of God.

Authentic faith

Prayer cannot change the unalterable Truth, nor can prayer alone give us an understanding of Truth; but prayer, coupled with a fervent habitual desire to know and do the will of God, will bring us into all Truth. . . .

Faith is higher and more spiritual than belief. It is a chrysalis state of human thought, in which spiritual evidence, contradicting the testimony of material sense, begins to appear, and Truth, the ever-present, is becoming understood. Human thoughts have their degrees of comparison. Some thoughts are better than others. A belief in Truth is better than a belief in error, but no mortal testimony is founded on the divine rock. Mortal testimony can be shaken. Until belief becomes faith, and faith becomes spiritual understanding, human thought has little relation to the actual or divine.

Mary Baker Eddy, *Science and Health with Key to the Scriptures*, Boston, 1875, pp. 11, 297

MARGIAD EVANS

Margiad Evans thought that Emily Brontë's writings revealed the 'nature mystic becoming the spiritual' and tried to trace her progress from nature mysticism through religious mysticism to 'what I call universal and ultimate mysticism'. A similar process is observable in her own works.

What is religion?

In *Autobiography* there was religion but it was religion incomplete, it was the worship of nature and solitude, the worship perhaps of God's body and not the soul of God. That was written about ten years ago. As time passed and I was always surrounded with beauty, the religious feeling grew, I think, and I meditated more and more often on it. What is religion? I asked myself (for being an egotistical-epileptic I would never ask any other authority). What is religion? It is reverence, tenderness, love, joy and worship. Reverence, tenderness, love and worship I could have given to another human being; but not joy. There was this deep religious sense in me, but nothing on which to pour it out. No person and no faith fits it; therefore it may perhaps have been created by God to be given back to him?

Margiad Evans, *A Ray of Darkness*, London, 1952, pp. 15–16

IDA GÖRRES

Ida Görres often wrestled with the problem of reconciling loyalty to a particular Christian tradition with the riches of other churches and movements. As here, she was able to restate with due vigour the need for diversity within unity.

River and tributaries

Diversity of tongues. It hurts to feel how monoglot we've become in the Church and what an obstacle it is. It's my most ardent wish to break up the pack-ice somehow, to help to bring about understanding. Of course systematized doctrine is the river, the central stream flowing through the land; but it must be able to catch up the wild torrents and streams rushing or trickling down from all sides, carrying these along with it on its way to the sea: otherwise it will dry up itself, and these waters work havoc or drain away to no purpose. But the estuaries are silted up, blocked. Père Couturier, the Dominican artist, saw the Church as a tall tree, bearing leaves only at the top, while one great branch after another – Eastern, German, English spirituality – is torn away in the course of history. For me this picture is too tragic in its immobility. I prefer to stick to my own image of the river and the tributaries, hoping that the connecting channels of these other streams, alien but clamouring to flow into the great river, can once again be cleared.

Ida Friederike Görres, *Broken Lights*, tr. B. Waldstein-Wartenberg, London, 1964, p. 299

LUCY HUTCHINSON

In her Memoirs *and verse Lucy Hutchinson presents her husband as a Puritan saint who must suffer the trials of prison and rigorous Bible study before he can become truly godly. Authentic piety required not meticulous adherence to the tenets of one true Church, but constant examination of a continually informed conscience. It has been remarked that Lucy Hutchinson is an example of how seventeenth-century women writers managed to assert their individuality as women with their own consciences and beliefs within a conventional model of inferiority and sub-mission to men. Her comparison of the birth of the Church from Christ's wounds to the creation of Eve from Adam's rib reveals the limitations of Puritan egalitarianism.*

So from the second Adam's bleeding side
God form'd the Gospel Church, his mystic Bride,
Whose strength was only of his firmness made,
His blood, quick spirits into ours convey'd:
His wasted flesh our wasted flesh supplied,
And we were then revived when he died.

Lucy Hutchinson, *Order and disorder: or, the world made and undone. Being meditations upon the creation and the fall; as it is recorded in the beginning of Genesis*, London, 1679, p. 38

KATHERINE PARR

In this passage from her Lamentation *Katherine stresses the importance of a 'lively', or constantly dynamic and aware, and 'justifying' faith of the Lutheran hue recommended, with vari-ous emphases, by Latimer, Tyndale and Cranmer. Although the individual is absolutely dependent on God for inspiration and direction, Katherine insists that her faith must be constantly and consciously renewed in the awareness and practice of love in order to receive God's enabling grace.*

A lively faith

I know, O my Lord, your eyes look upon my faith. Saint Paul says we are justified by the faith in Christ, and not by the deeds of the law. For if righteousness comes by the law, then Christ died in vain. Saint Paul means not here a dead human, historical faith, gotten by human industry, but a divine and lively faith which works by charity, as he himself plainly expresses. This dignity of faith is no derogation to good works, for out of this faith spring all good works. Yet we may not impute to the worthiness of faith or works our justification before God, but ascribe and give the worthiness of it wholly to the merits of Christ's passion, and refer and attribute the knowledge and perceiving thereof only to faith.

Katherine Parr, *Lamentation of a Sinner*, London, 1547

DOROTHY L. SAYERS

Dorothy L. Sayers was usefully alive to changes in attitude, and could draw a lesson from them.

Fear and courage

Few things are more striking than the change which has taken place during my own lifetime in the attitude of the intelligentsia towards the spokesmen of Christian opinion. When I was a child, bishops expressed doubts about the Resurrection, and were called courageous. When I was a girl, G. K. Chesterton professed belief in the Resurrection, and was called whimsical. When I was at college, thoughtful people expressed belief in the Resurrection 'in a spiritual sense', and were called advanced; (any other kind of belief was called obsolete, and its professors were held to be simple minded). When I was middle-aged, a number of lay persons, including some poets and writers of popular fiction, put forward rational arguments for the Resurrection, and were called courageous. Today, any lay apologist for Christianity, who is not a clergyman and whose works are sold and read, is liable to be abused in no uncertain terms as a mountebank, a reactionary, a tool of the Inquisition, a spiritual snob, an intellectual bully, an escapist, an obstructionist, a psychopathic introvert, an insensitive extravert, and an enemy of society. The charges are not always mutually compatible, but the common animus behind them is unmistakable, and its name is fear. Writers who attack these domineering Christians are called courageous.

Dorothy L. Sayers, *The Poetry of Search and the Poetry of Statement*, London, 1963, p. 69

ST EDITH STEIN

Knowing that 'God is the truth and whoever seeks the truth seeks God, whether he or she is fully aware of this or not', conceiving of striving towards God as a voyage into the soul, for 'we are drawn upward by turning inward', and sensing that the Holy Spirit was 'nearer to me than I to myself', Edith Stein often wrestled with uncertainty and mystery as functions of faith.

God's secret

What we believe we understand about our own soul is, after all, only a fleeting reflection of what will remain God's secret until the day all will be made manifest. My great joy consists in the hope of that future clarity. Faith in the secret history must always strengthen us when what we actually perceive (about ourselves or about others) might discourage us.

Letter no. 320, in *Self-Portrait in Letters, 1916–1942*, tr. Josephine Koeppel, in *Collected Works of Edith Stein*, vol. V; also in Sarah Borden, *Edith Stein*, London, 2003, p. 121

ANNA WHITE

Anna White belonged to the now all but extinct Christian community that forswore marriage and procreation. She was one of the few Shakers who wrote, and produced works on the meaning and message of Shakerism and on the motherhood of God. Here she states simply and clearly the theory of Christ's presence in the true believer.

The manifesting Spirit

We have taught through the years that the manifesting spirit of God – the Christ of the Ages – incarnates wherever man or woman with sincere purpose, honest effort and faithful obedience lives a pure life, and in self-denial and devotion to others becomes by self-effort and spiritual baptism at one with God.

Robert Edward Whitson, ed., *The Shakers: Two Centuries of Spiritual Reflection*, Mahwah, NY, 1984, p. 85

Prayer and Rapture

ə❧

ANGELA OF FOLIGNO

Angela describes the three kinds of prayer, physical, mental and
supernatural, apart from which she claims it is impossible to find
God.

Three kinds of prayer

Since it is necessary to know the uncreated God and Christ crucified, for otherwise we cannot transform our minds through divine
love, we should read diligently in the Book of Life, that is to say,
the life and death of Jesus Christ. We cannot possibly manage
this reading, or acquire this knowledge, without devout, pure,
humble, fervent, attentive, and constant prayer (not with the lips
alone, but with the heart and mind, and with all our strength).

We discover God through and in prayer. There are various
kinds of prayer, but God is to be found in three kinds: physical,
mental, and supernatural prayer.

Physical prayer is always accompanied by the sound of words
and by bodily exercises, such as kneeling down, asking forgiveness, and bowing down. I continually pray like that because,
sometimes, when I wanted to engage in mental prayer, I was
deceived and hindered by laziness and sleepiness, which made
me lose valuable time. And so I practise physical prayer, which
leads me towards the mental kind. But this must be done very
attentively. Therefore, when you say the Our Father, think very
carefully about exactly what you are saying, and don't repeat

it rapidly in order to make sure that you've said it this or that number of times, as is the practice of certain vain women who do good deeds for a reward.

Mental prayer occurs when meditation about God fills the mind so completely that it thinks about nothing other than God. But when some other reflection enters the mind, mental prayer is inappropriate because it prevents the tongue from doing its work, and it can't speak. In mental prayer the mind is so entirely filled with God that it can concern itself with nothing else, and thinks of nothing but God. In this way, mental leads to supernatural prayer.

Supernatural prayer is the kind during which the soul is so exalted by the knowledge of, or meditation on, or fulness of God that it is raised above its own nature until it understands more of God than it could manage otherwise, that is, naturally. When the soul understands, it knows; but it cannot explain what it knows, because all that it perceives and feels is above its own nature.

It is in these three degrees of prayer, therefore, that people learn to know God and themselves. Through knowing God, they love him, and when they love him they want to possess him. This is the sign of love, for anyone who loves not only a part of himself or herself, but the whole, is transformed in the course of loving and within that which is loved. . . .

Liber visionum (*Book of Divine Consolation*), Book XX, Alcalá, 1502

ST CATHERINE OF GENOA

Catherine of Genoa's accounts of mystical intensity have become classic descriptions of extreme spiritual states of mind.

Divine refreshment

Finding herself in such ardour, she felt herself compelled to turn to a figure of the Samaritan woman at the well with her Lord; and in her extreme distress Catherine addressed him thus: 'O Lord, I pray you, give me a little drop of this water, which of old you gave to the Samaritan woman, since I can no longer bear so great a fire.' And suddenly, in that instant, she was given a little drop of that divine water; and she was refreshed by it within and without, and was able to rest for some appreciable time.

Friedrich von Hügel, *The Mystical Element of Religion as Studied in Saint Catherine of Genoa and Her Friends*, vol. I, London, 1908, pp. 188–9

LUCIE CHRISTINE

God talks to Lucie Christine not as some distant concept but as someone who sympathizes intimately with her difficulties. When she is especially depressed by other people's lack of interest in her, or by their harshness or disdain, God comforts her 'inwardly' with the words: 'My dear daughter, there is nothing apart from you and me.' She answers: 'But what about other people, Lord?' He reassures her: 'As far as every single soul in this world is concerned, only you and I are here now. What can they do about it? After all, other souls and things exist only through me and in me!'

Dialogue with Christ

Dear Lord, you have shown me your divinity as something like a vitally luminous substance surrounding my whole being and holding it fast, yet simultaneously coursing through me and illuminating and enlightening me entirely. My soul has been resting in you, my Beloved, distinct from the world roundabout and enclosed wholly within you, living by virtue of you as you are you. The whole creation otherwise is silent when your love compels you, divine Lord, utter tenderness as you are, to let your poor creature know you in this way. . . .

Not long after communion I suddenly realized how everything exists in God. I watched a quite pure and powerful stream spring from a mountainside and pour its riches on the earth. Then it divided into an infinity of tiny rivulets and trickles. They were more or less clear or clouded, depending on the ground over and through which they flowed. So many people were there, looking for water, but very few went to the source itself to drink and draw their supplies. It was as if I saw all this in a single second. Jesus said to me: 'Do you see how people rush to these slimy, grubby little streams to quench their thirst, instead of climbing the mountain to reach the pure, unsullied source of all water? I contain all things in perfection. You will find everything in me if you abandon everything else for my sake.'

Lucie Christine, *Journal spirituel*, 4–18 September 1882, ed. P. A. Poulain SJ, Paris, 1916

DHUODA

Dhuoda offers her son surprisingly modern advice on his prayer-life.

Reverence in prayer

Reverence is what we offer something worthy of respect, which we must seek out with the deep feeling of the heart and the clear force of reason. If we seek of a man with great earthly power that he give us something useful, whether it be large or small, we seek this not with arrogance or loud protest or complaint, but we ask for it with all humility, so that he may command that what we seek be given. How much the more must we pray with respect to the founder and benefactor of all good things when we ask, seek, and find. Not in a loud voice nor in a lengthy speech but in deep and spontaneous feeling, in silence, we must seek of him that he give to us, endow us, enrich us, and deign to grant what we ask. In ancient times the holy Fathers prayed at great length and attained steadfast devotion in their pure petition. Why? Because in their great merits they were always with the Lord. . . .

Pray with your mouth, cry out with your heart, ask in your deeds that God come to your aid always, day and night, in every hour and every moment. As you lie quiet in bed, say three times: O God, come to my assistance. O Lord, make haste to help me, and then 'gloria' up to the end. Then say the Lord's Prayer. When that is done, say: 'Keep watch over me, Lord, throughout the day, and guard me in this night if such is your will. . . .'

Dhuoda, *Handbook for William: A Carolingian Woman's Counsel for Her Son*, tr. Carol Neel, Washington, DC, 1991, pp. 17–18

DOROTHY DAY

Dorothy Day describes her attitude to prayer with the brio for which she was famous, and which enraged hidebound, conventional Catholics when applied to social conditions.

Prayer and exultation

I am surprised that I am beginning to pray daily. I began because I had to. I just found myself praying. I can't get down on my knees, but I can pray while walking. If I get down on my knees, I think, 'Do I really believe? Whom am I praying to?' And a terrible doubt comes over me, and a sense of shame, and I wonder if I am praying because I am lonely, because I am unhappy.

But when I am walking up to the village for the mail, I find myself praying again, holding the rosary in my pocket that Mary Gordon gave me in New Orleans two years ago.

Then I think suddenly, scornfully, 'Here you are in a stupor of content. You are biological. Like a cow. Prayer with you is like the opiate of the people.' And over and over again in my mind that phrase is repeated jeeringly, 'Religion is the opiate of the people.'

'But,' I reason with myself, 'I am praying because I am happy, not because I am unhappy. I did not turn to God in unhappiness, in grief, in despair, to get consolation, to get something from him.'

And encouraged that I am praying because I want to thank him, I go on praying. No matter how dull the day, how long the walk seems, if I feel low at the beginning of the walk, the words I have been saying have insinuated themselves into my heart before

I have done, so that on the trip back I neither pray nor think but am filled with exultation.

Deborah Kent, *Dorothy Day: Friend of the Forgotten*, New York, 1996, pp. 47–8

MARY BAKER EDDY

One of the most influential aspects of Mrs Eddy's message was that disease and sin are illusions of mortal sense, and that the prayer of spiritual understanding under the guidance of God as supreme Mind can banish such imperfections.

God is all in all

Our Master taught his disciples one brief prayer, which we name after him the Lord's Prayer. Our Master said, 'After this manner therefore pray ye,' and then he gave that prayer which covers all human needs. . . .

Only as we rise above all material sensuousness and sin, can we reach the heaven-born aspiration and spiritual consciousness, which is indicated in the Lord's Prayer and which instantaneously heals the sick.

Here let me give what I understand to be the spiritual sense of the Lord's Prayer:

Our Father which art in heaven,
Our Father-Mother God, all-harmonious,
   Hallowed be Thy name.
Adorable One.
   Thy kingdom come.
Thy kingdom is come; Thou art ever-present.
   Thy will be done in earth, as it is in heaven.
Enable us to know, – as in heaven, so on earth, – God is omnipotent, supreme.
   Give us this day our daily bread;
Give us grace for to-day; feed the famished affections;
   And forgive us our debts, as we forgive our debtors.

And Love is reflected in love;

    And lead us not into temptation, but deliver us from evil;

And God leadeth us not into temptation, but delivereth us from sin, disease, and death.

    For Thine is the kingdom, and the power, and the glory, forever.

For God is infinite, all-power, all Life, Truth, Love, and all, and All.

Mary Baker Eddy, *Science and Health with Key to the Scriptures*, Boston, 1875, pp. 16–17

JEANNE-MARIE BOUVIER DE LA MOTTE-GUYON

Madame Guyon believed that the will could be moulded by prayerful practices until the conscious mind was beneficially overcome by God's all-powerful inspiration. Her autobiography gives some idea of the mixed experiences that shaped her spiritual development.

Prayer and privation

I read the works of St Francis and the life of Madame de Chantal. There I first learned what mental prayer was, and I besought my confessor to teach me that kind of prayer. As he did not, I used my own endeavours to practise it, though without success, as I then thought, because I could not exercise the imagination. I persuaded myself, that that prayer could not be made without forming to oneself certain ideas and reasoning much. This difficulty gave me no small trouble, for a long time. I was very assiduous and prayed earnestly to God to give me the gift of prayer. All that I saw in the life of Mme de Chantal charmed me. I was so much a child, that I thought I ought to do everything I saw in it. All the vows she had made, I made also. One day as I was reading that she had put the name of Jesus on her heart, to follow the counsel, 'set me as a seal upon thy heart'. For this purpose she had taken a hot iron, whereupon the holy name was engraven. I was very much afflicted that I could not do the same. I decided to write that sacred and adorable name, in large characters, on paper, then with ribbons and a needle I fastened it to my skin in four places. In that position it continued for a long time. . . .

About this time I fell into a state of total privation which lasted nearly seven years. I seemed to myself cast down like Nebuchadnezzar, to live among the beasts; a deplorable state, yet of the greatest advantage to me, by the use which divine wisdom made of it. This state of emptiness, darkness, and impotency, went far beyond any trials I had ever yet met . . . .

The only way to heaven is prayer; a prayer of the heart, which everyone is capable of, and not of reasonings which are the fruits of study, or exercise of the imagination, which in filling the mind with wandering objects, rarely settle it; instead of warming the heart with love of God, they leave it cold and languishing. Let the poor come, let the ignorant and carnal come; let the children without reason or knowledge come, let the dull or hard hearts which can retain nothing come to the practice of prayer and they shall become wise.

Mme Guyon, *Autobiography*, tr. T. T. Allen, London, 1897, vol. I, chs 4, 5, 21

CARYLL HOUSELANDER

In January 1953 Caryll Houselander wrote to a friend with a nervous illness to explain how prayer need not be 'mental' or exhaustingly formal.

Practical prayer

You say, 'I cannot pray, or concentrate, or paint' (when you are upset). Well . . . let your prayer be simply your offering of yourself to do God's will, to rest and relax in him, and to offer everything you do as a prayer; for example, if you have a little sleep, offer that; offer each mouthful of food that you eat, offer whatever you suffer, but all this simply and without any attempt at a formal offering in words or any kind of meditation or thinking about God.

Actually this kind of prayer that I propose to you brings you closer to God than anything you can say or think yourself, because it breaks down every barrier between you and God, every shred of resistance to his will, and allows him to speak to you, to hold you in his hand and surround you with his love. You imagine God to be far away from you, but really he is so close that you can't see him, like a child can't see her mother's face, if the mother is pressing her to her heart.

Now you ask how to spend the time to the best advantage mentally and physically as well as spiritually. As dressing dolls does absorb you, and I know how exquisitely you do it, I should certainly go on doing it. You might also interest yourself in making other toys, especially soft ones that you can sew, teddy bears, all sorts of cuddly animals, etc., especially with clothes to take on and off. I think all teddy bears need knitted suits. . . .

I would also advise you to make your own little indoor garden in your room, with a window box, and a few pots, or even a tub with a rose tree in it. . . .

The Letters of Caryll Houselander: Her Spiritual Legacy, ed. Maisie Ward, London and New York, 1973, pp. 214–16

KATHERINE PARR

One of the original prayers printed at the end of Katherine's Prayers or Meditations in 1545 was probably written to ask God's protection for the realm of England and, more especially, for the troops on their way to France, in summer 1544. She was then Queen Regent of a country at war, Henry being away to conduct the siege of Boulogne. It is a prayer of direct and simple petitions in the new reformed style, and a suitable accompaniment to Cranmer's new English Litany, composed at the same time and for the same occasion.

Prayer for men to say entering into battle

O Almighty King and Lord of hosts, who by your angels there-unto appointed ministers both war and peace, and who gave unto David both courage and strength, being but a little one, unarmed, and inexpert in feats of war, with his sling to set upon and over-throw the great huge Goliath: our cause now being just, and being forced to enter into war and battle, we most humbly beseech you (O Lord of hosts) so to turn the hearts of our enemies to the desire of peace, that no Christian blood be spilled, or else grant (O Lord) that with small effusion of blood, and to the little hurt and damage of innocents, we may to your glory obtain victory: and that the wars being soon ended, we may all with one heart and mind, knit together in concord and unity, laud and praise you: who lives and reigns, world without end. Amen.

Katherine Parr, *Prayers*, London, 1545

EVELYN UNDERHILL

In a piece originally written at Advent 1940, at a time of great national trial and anxiety, Evelyn Underhill stresses the impor-tance of an everyday quietism in Christian living.

Waiting not striving

We should think of the whole power and splendour of God as always pressing in on our small souls . . . but that power and splendour mostly reach us in homely inconspicuous ways; in the sacraments, and in our prayers, joys, and sorrows and in all opportunities of loving service. This means that one of the most important things in our prayer is the eagerness and confidence with which we throw ourselves open to his perpetual coming. There should always be more waiting than striving in a Christian prayer.

M. Cropper, *Life of Evelyn Underhill*, London, 1958, p. 218

MARY WARD

Mary's vocation and direction seem to have been revealed to her by degrees. From the age of fifteen she felt God was calling her to a religious life, but she had no idea what form it would take and which order she should join. She refused to marry Edward Neville, the future husband chosen for her, left England and became an 'out-sister' in the Convent of the Poor Clares in St-Omer. In her autobiography she tells how on St Athanasius' day (2 May) she sensed that God wanted her to leave the Order of St Clare. When she visited England in 1609 she had another intense experience of God guiding her towards her destiny.

Abstracted out of my being

One morning, making my meditation coldly, not at all to my satisfaction, at the end of it I resolved to assist a person to be accepted in some convent who much desired to become a nun, but, wanting a portion, could not otherwise enter one; and then going to dress myself according to the fashion of the country and other circumstances, whilst I adorned my head at the mirror, something very supernatural befell me, similar to that already related on the day of St Athanasius, but more singular, and, as it appears to me, with greater impetuosity, if greater there could be. I was abstracted out of my whole being, and it was shown to me with clearness and inexpressible certainty that I was not to be of the Order of St Teresa, but that some other thing was determined for me, without all comparison more to the glory of God than my entrance into that holy religion would be. I did not see what the assured good thing would be, but the glory of God which was to come through it, showed itself inexplicably and so abundantly as to fill my soul in such a way that I remained for a good space without feeling or hearing anything but the sound, 'Glory, glory, glory'. By accident I was then alone, therefore what external changes this and similar things cause I cannot say, but from the internal feeling and bodily disturbance they must be remarkable; my knowledge fails as to their continuance; all appears to last but a moment, even at those times when afterwards I made a computation of time, and found it to have been about two hours.

On this occasion a good space of time passed before I recovered; but, returned to myself, and finding my heart full of love for this thing, accompanied by such glory that not yet can I comprehend what it was, and seeing for certain that I was not to be of the Order of St Teresa, remembering also the vow that I had made of being of that Order if my confessor should command me, I felt great fear of offending God in these two contraries, or of adhering to one or the other side; to resist that which now had been operated in me I could not, and to have a will in opposition to the vow I ought not. In this conflict, giving myself to prayer, I protested to God, so liberal, that I had not and would not admit on this occasion any other will than his, and, as a testimony and sign that my mind and will were totally to do his without exception, I put on a hair-cloth, which I have forgotten for how long a time I wore, but I believe for some continuance, for I well recollect that through this and other corporal penances, done for this end during the months that I remained in England, I did no little injury to my health, especially being occupied at that time with some fervour in winning and aiding others.

Mother M. Salome, *Mary Ward: A Foundress of the 17th Century*, London, 1901, pp. 62–4

Illness and Transformation

⚜

MARY BAKER EDDY

Mrs Eddy believed that only mind exists and that matter, sin, disease and death are unreal. Creative faith can destroy these delusions and enable humans to approach perfection as the ultimate expression of mind.

Divine energy

Mortals develop their own bodies or make them sick, according as they influence them through mortal mind. . . . The feats of the gymnast prove that latent mental fears are subdued by him. The devotion of thought to an honest achievement makes the achievement possible. Exceptions only confirm this, proving that failure is occasioned by a too feeble faith. Had Blondin believed it impossible to walk the rope over Niagara's abyss of waters, he could never have done it. His belief that he could do it gave his thought-forces, called muscles, their flexibility and power which the unscientific might attribute to a lubricating oil. . . .

Let the 'male and female' of God's creating appear. Let us feel the divine energy of Spirit, bringing us into newness of life and recognizing no mortal nor material power as able to destroy. Let us rejoice that we are subject to the divine 'powers that be'.

Mary Baker Eddy, *Science and Health with Key to the Scriptures*, Boston, 1875, pp. 199, 249

CARYLL HOUSELANDER

In October 1953 Caryll Houselander wrote to advise a friend who had suffered a nervous breakdown not only that one can be mistaken about the 'right thing to do' but that times of powerlessness can have their own virtue.

Redeeming power

. . . I am very sorry to hear of your breakdown, but at the same time I think that if it was the only thing to stop you from sacrificing your very great creative gifts to nursing and ward-maiding, then it is something to be thankful for.

You are right, God gives one talents to use, not to crush – remember the parable of the talents? To have an art at your finger tips and in your mind, as you have, is a trust; you are meant to develop and use it, partly because it is only by doing so that you can fully integrate your own personality – and that is another way of saying 'save your soul' – and partly because you must give to the world, to the millions who are starved for beauty, the beauty that God has given into your trust for that purpose. . . .

No doubt, one who loved men as [Christ] did would have longed to heal all their sickness, to enlighten all their minds, to transform the world by miracle upon miracle of love, but God did not will that for him. On the contrary, he willed that he should be, humanly speaking, a failure, should be nailed to the cross and suffer there in helplessness. Indeed, the moment in which his love was consummated, in which the crisis of his redeeming power was reached, was when the hands that could heal with a touch were nailed back out of reach. . . .

The Letters of Caryll Houselander: Her Spiritual Legacy, ed. Maisie Ward, London and New York, 1973, pp. 216–77

LUCY HUTCHINSON

Lucy Hutchinson's prose and verse accounts of her saintly husband offer as one of his main virtues his reliance on the transforming light of the gospel, which in prison 'in his darkest solitude shot rays / That shamed the splendour of the brightest days' and enlightened him with truths 'which no glad mortal in / The free world meets'. She wants her children to realize the source of his virtues and she is careful to represent her husband as a man who was divinely led to the right wife.

The work of providence

Let not excess of love and delight in the stream make us forget the fountain; he and all his excellencies came from God, and flowed back into their own spring: there let us seek them, thither let us hasten after him; there having found him, let us cease to bewail among the dead that which is risen, or rather immortal. His soul conversed with God so much when he was here, that it rejoices to be now eternally freed from interruption in that blessed exercise; his virtues were recorded in heaven's annals, and can never perish; by them he yet teaches us and all those to whose knowledge they shall arrive. It is only his fetters, his sins, his infirmities, his diseases, that are dead never to revive again, nor would we have them; they were his enemies and ours; by faith in Christ he vanquished them . . . we should see him even in heaven, holding forth his flaming lamp of virtuous examples and precepts, to light us through the dark world. . . .

Mr Hutchinson was . . . invited to their houses, where he was nobly treated, with all the attractive arts that young women and their parents use to procure them lovers; but though some of them were very handsome, others wealthy, witty, and well qualified, and all of them set out with all the gaiety and bravery that vain women put on to set themselves off, yet Mr Hutchinson could not be entangled in any of their fine snares; but without any taint of incivility, he in such a way of handsome raillery reproved their pride and vanity, as made them ashamed of their glory, and vexed that he alone, of all the young gentlemen that belonged to the court or neighbourhood, should be insensible of their charms. . . . In the same house with him there was a younger daughter of Sir Allen Apsley . . . this gentlewoman . . . was a very child, her elder sister being at the time scarcely past it; but a child of such pleasantness and vivacity of spirit, and ingenuity in the quality she practised [music], that Mr Hutchinson took pleasure in hearing her practise, and would fall in discourse with her. She having the keys of her mother's house . . . would sometimes ask Mr Hutchinson, when she went over to walk along with her. One day when he was there, looking upon an odd by-shelf in her sister's closet, he found a few Latin books; asking whose they were, he was told they were her elder sister's . . . he grew to love to hear mention of her, and the other gentlewomen who had been her companions used to talk much to him of her, telling him how reserved and studious she was, and other things which they esteemed no advantage. But it so much inflamed Mr Hutchinson's desire of seeing her, that he began to wonder at himself, that his heart, which had ever entertained so much indifference for the most excellent of womankind, should have such strong impulses towards a stranger he never saw; and certainly it was of the Lord (though he perceived it not), who had ordained him, through so many various providences, to be yoked with her in whom he found so much satisfaction.

Lucy Hutchinson, *Memoirs of Colonel Hutchinson*, London, 1908, pp. 17–18, 45–6

MARIE LATASTE

The Jesuit poet Gerard Manley Hopkins, like many others all over the world, found Marie Lataste's writings fresh and original and intellectually strong and sure. Hopkins was particularly impressed by Marie's report of a private revelation that God moves the world in two ways: creatively, according to the nature of things; and redemptively, according to personal choice. Marie seems to have happened upon the same point that Scotus made

*about predestination; even if no one had ever sinned, some kind
of redemption or sacrifice by Christ would have been necessary
to provide the opportunity for love by free choice. Hopkins also
saw in her works evidence of the ways in which God's design is
worked out in nature by 'stress' and 'instress', as in human minds
and wills. He will certainly have recognized the ways in which
Marie's personal pious inclinations were constrained – though
far from entirely – by her priestly correspondent's insistence on
the primacy of ecclesiastical instruction and the untrustworthi-
ness of the religion of the heart.*

Some extraordinary things that happened to me

One Sunday, at the beginning of Mass, the Saviour Jesus made
me repeat the Confiteor and the Act of Contrition. After this, he
gave me absolution of all my sins. Then he said 'Let a robe dyed
in the chalice of my blood be brought hither, a veil dipped in the
water of the Divinity, and a crown wrought by the Holy Ghost
himself. I wish her to be clothed today as one of the princesses of
heaven'. His orders were obeyed. There were brought a red robe,
a veil of dazzling brightness, and a crown of white flowers, the
like to which I have never seen. When I was arrayed therein, my
face, and my hands, and feet became of a shining whiteness, and
Jesus made me sit on a low seat by his side. I had a golden girdle
round my loins, and I felt unspeakably happy. At the elevation
I heard the Saviour address some words to the faithful, and tell
them that it was for love of them he had descended from heaven
to dwell on the altar, and in the tabernacle.

After communion I opened the little door of my heart, which
was like a small chamber, very fair and pleasant; Jesus entered
therein, and seated himself on the throne of which I have already
spoken. I remained there, near Jesus, with my guardian angel and
the blessed Virgin, who had entered in with us. I remained thus
arrayed the whole day, abiding in the interior of my heart. . . .

From my infancy I was taught that there was a God, that I
must attach myself to him, that I must adore him, love him, and
serve him; and I tried to know him, to love him, and to serve him.

Now, it was in seeking God and in loving him that I experienced all that I have stated in my papers and in my letters. In order not to continue to experience it, I must separate myself from God. It is from him, then, that all has proceeded. Never will I separate myself from him, unless this God who was made known to me in my childhood, and in whom I have experienced all that I have related, is not the true God, but is rejected by the Church. If it be so, I renounce this God for the God of the Church, Catholic, Apostolic, and Roman. I will refuse him all my adorations, and regard all that he has told me as needing, in order to [confirm] my belief in it, to be modified by the teachings of the Church. I desire to follow no other leading. But I know very well that there is no other God save the God of my heart, the God whom I know, and whom I love with my whole soul. It is he who has taught me all, it is he who is the principle of all which I have committed to you, it is from him that I received it. These writings, therefore, must be good, like everything which comes from God.

If I consider them in their end, I still say that they come from God, because the end of these writings is good; it would not be so if they came from the devil. What, in fact, is the object of the writings which I have committed to you? The glory of God, the salvation of my soul, and the salvation of the souls of my brethren. Indeed everything therein speaks of giving glory to God and submitting to his will; everything leads souls to him, attaches them to him, and engages them to love and serve him faithfully.

Letters and Writings of Marie Lataste, tr. Edward Healy Thompson, London, 1894, vol. III, pp. 37–8, 151–2

Abandonment and the
Dark Night of the Soul

⁂

AGNES BEAUMONT

The persecuted Agnes Beaumont asks for strength to overcome dejection and loneliness, and to face her tormentors even if the greatest physical endurance is called for, and later ascribes her deliverance to God's influence on the human mind and conscience. Burning at the stake was the punishment to be expected at that time by a woman who was found guilty of treason, or of murdering her husband or father.

Into a corner by myself

So that day the coroner was to come in the afternoon, some of the Gamgy friends came to me, and they spent several hours in prayer before the coroner came, that God would please to appear graciously for me, and for the glory of his name. So when they had done, I got into a corner by myself; for I had a great mind, to be with God alone at the throne of grace where I usually found relief, and succour, and help. And that was very much upon my heart, to cry to the Lord to give me his presence that day; so much of it that I might not have a dejected countenance, nor be of a daunted spirit before them; for I see that to be brought before a company of men, and to come before them of being accused of murdering my own father, that, although I knew myself clear in the sight of God, yet without a boundance of his presence, I should sink before them. Thought I, if they should see me dejected and look daunted, they would think I was guilty. I begged the Lord that he would please to carry me above the fears of men, and devils, and death itself; and that he would give me faith and courage that I might look my accuser in the face with boldness, and that I might lift up my head before him, with conviction to themselves. I stood before them . . . all the jury was much concerned for me, though carnal men, and it was observed they sat with wet eyes many of them while the coroner was examining me. And indeed I had cause to thank God, that he did convince them of my innocence. And I heard that a twelvemonth after they would speak of me with tears.

The Narrative of the Persecution of Agnes Beaumont: A Diary, ed. G. B. Harrison, London, n.d., pp. 73–5, 85

DHUODA

Dhuoda gives her son advice on times when he might feel abandoned by God.

Times of abandonment

If you are afflicted by various trials and constrained on all sides by human or spiritual temptations, if you feel abandoned by God – who in this way abandons many of his saints in order to test them – and if in this trouble you seem to face a temptation greater than you can bear, recite within your own spirit those Psalms that begin God, my God, look upon me, Hear, O God, my supplication, Hear, O God, my prayer when I make supplication to thee, and Save me, O Lord; and he will come to your aid immediately, so that you can endure the temptation that you suffer.

If your earthly life weighs upon you, if your spirit finds delight in contemplating your heavenly fatherland and looking upon omnipotent God with burning desire, recite these Psalms with an attentive spirit: As the hart, How lovely . . . Lord, My God to thee at break of day; and the merciful God will swiftly console your mind.

If you feel that you have been abandoned by God in your trials, recite these psalms with a contrite heart: How long, O Lord, O God, with our ears, Have mercy on me, O God, Hear, O God, my prayer and despise not, In you, O Lord, have I hoped; and God at once will make you happy in all your hardships.

Dhuoda, *Handbook for William: A Carolingian Woman's Counsel for Her Son*, tr. Carol Neel, Washington, DC, 1991, pp. 104–5

DOROTHY DAY

Dorothy Day never hid the emotional content of the determination that carried her through the most daunting extremes of opposition to her schemes for the support, education and regeneration of the poor and marginalized.

Only the will remains

'Are we trying to make a farm here, or aren't we?' A statement of that kind, an attitude of criticism of all that Peter and I stand for, has the power to down me completely. . . . Nothing but the grace of God can help me, but I feel utterly lacking, ineffective. . . .

I have had this completely alone feeling. A temptation of the devil, doubtless, and to succumb to it is a lack of faith and hope. There is nothing to do but bear it, but my heart is as heavy as lead, and my mind dull and uninspired. A time when the memory and understanding fail one completely and only the will remains, so that I feel hard and rigid, and at the same time ready to sit like a soft fool and weep.

Deborah Kent, *Dorothy Day: Friend of the Forgotten*, New York, 1996, p. 100

HADEWIJCH

Either Hadewijch or, more probably, one of her later Beguine followers in the same tradition ('Pseudo-Hadewijch' or 'the second Hadewijch'), writes of the soul's experiences as it tries to recover its lost likeness to God in infinite simplicity or 'spiritual nakedness'.

The poor in spirit

Naked love which spares nothing
In its wild death
When every accident is left aside
Finds itself again pure essence.

In love's pure abandon
No created good can subsist:
For love strips of all form
Those whom it receives in its simplicity.

Freed from every modality,
Alien to every image
Is the life here below
Of the poor in spirit.

All is not found in poverty,
Exile and all such ways:
The poor in spirit must dwell
Without notions in a vast simplicity,

A simplicity without end, and having no beginning
Neither form, modality, reason, nor object,
Without opinion, or thought, or intention, or learning:
One that is boundless and without any limit.

Here in this wild desert
Dwell in unity the poor in spirit.
Nothing is there for them save freedom in a silence
Ever answering to Eternity.

Hadewijch, *Mengeldichten*, xxvi, in J. Leclercq et al., *The Spirituality of the Middle Ages*, London, 1968, pp. 362–3

HILDEGARD OF BINGEN

From a very early age Hildegard was aware that she possessed a unique power of 'perception' and knew that 'If human beings ask no questions, the Holy Spirit gives no answers.' Many people didn't understand her and were slow to appreciate her special gifts.

Perception

At first, if my visionary insight seized me and flowed through me with all its power, I would speak out and start telling people one thing after the other that I had seen, but they soon made it quite obvious that they found my behaviour very odd indeed. This made me ashamed of what was happening to me. I used to cry a lot and reached the point where I desperately wanted to say absolutely nothing about it all. But, somehow, that just wasn't possible. All the same, I was so afraid of other people's reactions that, although I couldn't stop myself saying that I saw things, I took care to say nothing about *how* I saw them.

Vita Sanctae Hildegardis in *Patrologia Latina*, Vol. 197, tr. J. Cumming, Paris, 1882, c. 115

FLORENCE NIGHTINGALE

Florence Nightingale evoked very different opinions from contemporaries and later critics. The novelist Mrs Gaskell thought her 'completely led by God as Joan of Arc. . . . it makes one feel the livingness of God more than ever to think how straight he is sending his spirit down into her, as into the prophets and saints of old'.

Lytton Strachey, however, remarked that her conception of God was 'certainly not orthodox. She felt towards him as she might have felt towards a glorified sanitary engineer . . . one has the impression that Miss Nightingale has got the Almighty too into her clutches, and that, if he is not careful, she will kill him with overwork.' Half a century later, for Ida Görres, the practical achievements of Nightingale surpassed making up 'spiritual posies', and stressing the supernatural to avoid facing reality. She was a 'glorious embodiment of the best of the nineteenth century – with its enthusiasm for Progress in all its pristine freshness', and a really great woman, 'boundless in magnanimity, with her flaming, insatiable Eros-nature. . . . Is all this not more than if she had turned her back on men in total renunciation, tying up her will in obedience, perhaps under a narrow and incompetent superior, robbing herself through poverty of most of the chances to help and give pleasure? And did she not still live up to all three evangelical counsels, and on a heroic scale at that: virginity, forgoing the cravings of the heart again and again for the sake of her vocation; obedience, to its wearing, merciless claims; poverty, in the austere and selfless privations involved in her utter surrender to the "one thing needful"? Is her broad, glowing, generous Christianity not more truly human, more truly Christian than at least our present-day cloister ideal?' (Broken Lights, London, 1964, pp. 148–50).

In 1850–1 Florence Nightingale wrote in her diary:

What am I?

I am 30 . . . the age at which Christ began his mission. No more childish things, no more vain things, no more love, no more marriage. Now, Lord, let me only think of thy will.

My present life is suicide; in my 31st year I see nothing desirable but death; What am I that their life is not good enough for me? Oh God what am I? The thoughts and feelings that I have now I can remember since I was six years old. It was not I that made them. . . . But why, oh my God, cannot I be satisfied with the life that satisfies so many people?

Ruth Y. Jenkins, *Reclaiming Myths of Power: Women Writers and the Victorian Spiritual Crisis*, London and New York, 1996, pp. 53–4

DOROTHY L. SAYERS

Dorothy L. Sayers had an extraordinary ability to present great Christian truths in short, pithy statements.

Divine transformation

God did not abolish the fact of evil: He transformed it. He did not stop the crucifixion: He rose from the dead.

A Matter of Eternity: Selections from the Writings of Dorothy L. Sayers, ed. Rosamond Kent Sprague, London, 1973, p. 12

ST THÉRÈSE OF LISIEUX

The Abbé Maurice Bellière, an aspiring missionary, was Thérèse's first 'spiritual brother'. She corresponded with him and prayed for him during the last two years of her life. She echoes Old Testament passages and the writings of mystics when she says in this letter of 1896 that God tests his disciples.

Saving grace

The fact is that when Jesus calls a man to guide and save multitudes of souls, it is most necessary that he should make him experience the temptations and trials of life. Since he has given you the grace to come forth victorious from the struggle, I hope, Monsieur l'Abbé, that our sweet Jesus will fulfil your great desires. I ask him that you may be, not a good missionary merely, but a saint, all aflame with love for God and love for souls. Obtain that love for me too, I beg, that I may help you in your apostolic labour. You know that a Carmelite who was not an apostle would be losing sight of the goal of her vocation and would cease to be a daughter of the Seraphic St Teresa, who would have given a thousand lives to save a single soul.

Collected Letters of St Thérèse of Lisieux, tr. F. J. Sheed, London and New York, 1948, p. 255–6

Truth and Simplicity

❦

MARIE BASHKIRTSEFF

In her journal Marie Bashkirtseff scrupulously recorded her dreams, ambitions, fears, faults and struggle to achieve something worthwhile yet come to terms with impending death. In one sense, her journal is also an account of a lifelong developing acknowledgement of self and a simultaneous escape not only from the conventions imposed by family and rank but from the restrictions of the very egotistical desire that seems to promise liberation. Her extraordinary frankness has inspired countless writers and philosophers, such as Katherine Mansfield and Bernard Berenson (to cite two very different examples).

Truth-telling

Why should I lie and dissemble? Yes, it is true that I wish, if not hope, to remain on this earth in some shape or form. If I don't die young, then I hope to stay alive as a great artist. But if I do die young I should like to have my journal published, for surely it must be of interest. But you will object that when I talk of publication, the very thought that people will read what I write detracts from – well, actually, must totally destroy – the specific purpose of this kind of book. But no, for, first of all, I have written for some time without any thought of anyone reading what I say, and then, precisely because I hope to be read at some time, that means that I am being absolutely honest, doesn't it? If this book isn't the exact, absolute, strict truth, it has no justification. I not only always say what I think, but never for a single moment have I thought of concealing anything that makes me look ridiculous or is to my disadvantage. Anyway I think too much of myself to be parsimonious with the truth about myself. Yes, dear readers, you may rest assured that I display myself relentlessly in these pages. You will probably find my particular ego of scarcely any special interest, but what you must do is to think of me instead as a human being in a famous novel relating everything that has happened to him or her from infancy. Then, I think, you will find my testimony enthralling. Just ask writers like Emile Zola, Edmond de Goncourt and even Guy de Maupassant whether that's worthwhile! On the other hand, my journal begins when I'm twelve and I now find that it starts to say something truly worth saying only when I reach fifteen or sixteen. That indicates some kind of inadequacy, I suppose, so I am writing something in the nature of a prologue to help you understand the purpose of this great literary achievement.

All right then, let us suppose that I am famous enough to be read with deep interest. . . .

What would happen if I happened to die now, just as I am, because of some illness? . . . It could be that I am really in danger of dying and they just aren't telling me, and then when I'm dead they riffle through my drawers and find my journal. Then, after reading it, my family will destroy it and before long there will be nothing . . . nothing . . . yes, nothing at all left of me! . . . I've always found that difficult to accept. Life, so many ambitions, all that suffering, all those tears, and all that struggle, struggle, struggle, and in the end you're forgotten! . . . Just oblivion! . . . as if you'd never existed. But if I don't live enough of a life to become famous, at least this journal will be of some interest to students of human nature as the life of a woman, day by day, without any pretension, written as if no one was ever going to read it, and yet at the same time written to be read. That is rather unusual, isn't it? I'm sure, somehow, that people will find my personality congenial, because I say everything: I tell it all as it is. If I didn't, what would be the point of writing? You will soon appreciate, as you read on, how I leave nothing out. . . .

Marie Bashkirtseff, *Journal*, Paris, 1887, from the Prologue, 1 May 1884

EMILY DICKINSON

Emily Dickinson wittily restates the paradox that we have an inborn sense of belonging and an irresistible feeling of lostness.

If ever the lid . . .

If ever the lid gets off my head
And lets the brain away
The fellow will go where he belonged –
Without a hint from me,

And the world – if the world be looking on –
Will see how far from home
It is possible for sense to live
The soul there – all the time.

Publ. 1945; *The Complete Poems of Emily Dickinson*, ed. T. H. Johnson, London, 1970, p. 701

IDA GÖRRES

Although Ida Görres was noted for her uncompromising readiness to criticize received opinions and prejudices, she was well aware of the importance of compromise and of a form of submission that was far from cowardly.

The union of wills

How I'd like to write something comprehensive, really valid on . . . the real significance of the Law: not remotely, not in the faintest degree contrary to personal conscience – as voices keep insisting here, ever louder, ever more stridently decrying the Law as constraint, tyranny, distorting the voice of conscience, dead letter, convention, and all the rest of it. No, commandments, orders, decrees, ruling, bidding: psalm 118 is full of such weighty, massive words – and how gladly the soul responds in joyous surrender, ardently, tenderly – a bride, not a captive seized and raped. Yes, yes, and yes again, assent welling up from the innermost depths! But I suppose only someone who knows love can really understand this, who knows what it means to fuse with the will of the beloved, deliberately, of one's own volition, surrendering one's own will to his – someone who has really experienced the union of two wills.

Ida Friederike Görres, *Broken Lights*, tr. B. Waldstein-Wartenberg, London, 1964, pp. 83–4

CARYLL HOUSELANDER

Caryll Houselander points out the saving virtue of simple attitudes and demands.

Trust and humility

Simplicity is not – as so many think, and, alas, teach – silliness. Simplicity means not being complicated, not being double in any way, not deluding oneself or anyone else. The first exercise in simplicity is to accept oneself as one is.

There are two tremendous results of this: one is humility; the other is that it enables other people to accept us as we are, and in this there is real charity. People whose demand on others is simple and uncomplicated add to the life of the world. One of the main reasons for devitalization, depression and psychological tiredness is that we make complicated demands on one another. . . . Some people . . . exhaust us. Others make only the slightest demands, and others actually give. . . .

The individual who is simple, who accepts himself as he is, makes only a minimum demand on others in their relations with him. His simplicity not only endows his own personality with unique beauty; it is also an act of real love. This is an example of the truth that whatever sanctifies our own soul at the same time benefits everyone who comes into our life. . . . We cease to want to be rich, successful or popular, and want instead the things that satisfy our deeper instincts: to be at home, to make things with our hands, to have time to see and wonder at the beauty of the earth, to love and to be loved. . . . To accept oneself as one is; to accept life as it is: these are the two basic elements of childhood's simplicity and humility . . . we have not the least idea of the miracle of life-giving love that we are. There is no pretence that can approach the wonder of the truth about us, no unreality that comes anywhere near the reality. . . .

The acceptance of life as it is must teach us trust and humility. . . . If, in the light of this knowledge, we give ourselves unreservedly to life, every phase of it, every experience in it will lead us back to the inward heaven of spiritual childhood. . . .

Caryll Houselander, 'Giving Ourselves Unreservedly to Life', in *The Passion of the Infant Christ*, New York and London, 1949

LOUISA J. ROBERTS

This extract from Louisa J. Roberts' sermon is a classic example of Quaker women's preaching on the traditional theme of salvation: superbly paced, with well-balanced emphases in order to counter the notion of divine sacrifice held by the mainline churches.

What shall I do to be saved?

'What must I do to be saved?' This momentous question comes to every one of us, at some period of our lives, and becomes for the time the absorbing thought. When this question was put by the trembling, conscience-stricken jailer to the Apostle, the answer given was, 'Believe on the Lord Jesus Christ and thou shalt be saved.' This marks the first step towards salvation, and what this belief implies has been a subject of controversy during all the centuries that have passed since that time.

We find ourselves in danger outwardly, from which we see no way of escape, until there comes before us something that promises relief; we believe that relief can come to us through its agency, and we cry for help! We all have known this, and we all have known that unless we saw some hope of being saved from the impending calamity through the help of another, that if we had not believed this possible, we should have sunk under the calamity that threatened us. This is our outward experience, and it becomes plain to every one of us that if we are in need of help we must apply to those who can help us. If we are in danger of losing our lives we must turn to those who can save us from the peril that is before us. All spiritual relations are subject to the same laws of cause and effect that govern us in the outward world, and that which is outward becomes the type of that which is inward, spiritual, and eternal.

Now we come back to the thought of salvation by Christ; and that is the point that most concerns us in relation to this spiritual life of ours. What is it to be saved, – saved spiritually? It may be to be rescued from some danger into which we have plunged, it may be to be preserved from some danger that threatens us, into which we have not yet fallen; it is either to be taken out of the trouble or to be preserved from the danger which confronts us. And it is just here, as I apprehend, that the line of divergence comes when we speak of being saved by the Lord Jesus Christ, as the expression is given. Our Christian brethren of other persuasions, sincere and earnest as ourselves, have a 'scheme of salvation,' based upon the earlier thought of sacrifice, upon that idea which came into the world perhaps among the first religious thoughts of the human family, that we must offer something to the Power whose force and energy were seen through the phenomena of nature, but who was invisible to the eyes of men and must be appeased, must be made the friend of man through the offering of something he values as his greatest treasure. Thus he gave his first-born for the sins of his body; he gave the treasures of the field, the firstlings of his flocks and herds, and hoped thereby to gain the favour of the Power he feared. And so sacrifice came to be considered the way to salvation; and man was saved, brought into the highest favour, through what he offered of his treasures to the Divine Majesty.

As the years rolled on and the centuries passed, man began to see more clearly the basis upon which his acceptance rested, and some thought came to the foremost thinkers of the race that it was not by anything that man could offer outwardly that acceptance with God was gained, but that the fruit of his lips, the meditation of his heart, and the desires of his soul must be in harmony with that which was his highest conception of God to bring him to that peace which to be saved seems to imply. And so, down through the ages, as we come to the time of the manifestation in Judaea of the blessed Son . . . sent of the Father there was growing in the thoughts of men a more divine idea of salvation by sacrifice, and a preparing of the minds of many of the lowly ones of Israel for the salvation that was promised in the coming of the Messiah. And he in his coming and his teaching made this clear to all who were willing to free themselves from the traditions and usages by which the souls of men had been bound for all the centuries that had passed.

And there were a few humble, sincere ones who heard him gladly, for it was then as it is now, that only the simple-hearted were willing to accept the truth as he taught it, – the sorrowing ones seeking help, seeking rest for the weariness of the body, the weariness of the soul. He said to these, 'Come unto me all ye that labour and are heavy laden, and I will give you rest. Take my yoke upon you and learn of me,' – and here, precious friends, comes in the grand culminating thought – 'for I am meek and lowly in heart, and ye shall find rest for your souls.'

This is what he taught concerning the part that he has in the saving of the souls of men. And shall we go from him and his testimony to those who see in him the representation and type of all the forms and ceremonies, the offerings and sacrifices, from the first effort of man to be at peace with God down to the tragedy of the Cross? Shall we turn to this act – as the only means by which we may be saved? Shall we affirm that only as we believe him to have been God sacrificed for man, dying on the Cross to expiate the sins not only of those of his own time, but of all those who have lived before him, and all who would live afterward to the latest day of humanity upon earth, are we to hold that only as we believe this can we have any hope or any part in the great salvation?

Truth and Simplicity

O my friends, when my mind is turned to contemplate this perversion of the simple truth as it was in Jesus, of how men have laboured to make such a mystery of salvation that only the learned ones can follow the idea and reach to that which is real and lasting, when I think over it all, I feel like lifting up my heart in thankfulness that though the Apostle declared that not many of the learned and mighty ones have been called into the simplicity of the Gospel as taught by Jesus, it meets the want of every earnest, seeking soul, every soul that in meekness and lowliness of heart is following Jesus in the way of his coming to that soul; following him in all that relates to his intercourse with his fellow-men, following him in his intercourse with the Father, who, he declared, was not only Father, but our Father. That relationship makes Jesus our brother, not our God to be sacrificed by another part of himself that we might escape the punishment due our transgressions. O my friends, Jesus never so taught, and the instincts of our own souls if yielded to, the natural instincts that God has given to every one of us, revolt from the thought of being saved, through the sacrifice of the purest, holiest son of God that has ever walked the earth. The soul turns from the thought, and would rather bear its own iniquity, if it is true to the highest instincts that God has placed in the human heart, would rather bear its own iniquity than owe its salvation to the cruel, cruel scourging and death of the Immaculate One. And it is a precious thought, that brings gladness to my heart, that the world is rising out of this, and coming to understand what the believing in the Lord Jesus Christ is, which saves us.

A sermon by Louisa J. Roberts at Green Street Meeting, Philadelphia, 1889. From phonographic notes by Sue R. Wilkins, *Biographical Sketch of Louisa J. Roberts with Extracts from Her Journal and Selections from Her Writings*, Philadelphia, 1895, pp. 244–52

DOROTHY L. SAYERS

Dorothy L. Sayers was far from being an unredeemed traditionalist in matters religious and social, but could be curatively analytical when necessary.

Equality and progress

We cannot but be sharply struck by the fact that two of our favourite catch-words have absolutely no meaning in Heaven: there is no equality and there is no progress. Perhaps I should modify that a little: there is equality in the sense that all the souls alike are as full of bliss as they are capable of being: but between soul and soul there is no formal equality at all. The pint-pot and the quart-pot are equally full: but there is no pretence that a pint and a quart are the same thing; neither does the pint-pot ever dream of saying to the quart-pot, 'I'm as good as you are' – still less of saying 'It isn't fair that you should hold more than I'. The old sin of Envy, which unleashed the She-Wolf of Avarice from Hell, is utterly extinguished in Heaven. And here is no progress at all in the sense of 'bettering one's self' or 'getting even with other people'.

Dorothy L. Sayers, *Introductory Papers on Dante*, New York, 1957, p. 57

ELIZABETH CADY STANTON

Elizabeth Cady Stanton's 'Declaration' is a classic Christian statement of the inalienable God-given right of women to equality with men.

The Seneca Falls Declaration (1848)

When, in the course of human events, it becomes necessary for one portion of the family of man to assume among the people of the earth a position different from that which they have hitherto occupied, but one to which the laws of nature and of nature's God entitle them, a decent respect to the opinions of mankind requires that they should declare the causes that impel them to such a course. We hold these truths to be self-evident: that all men and women are created equal; that they are endowed by their Creator with certain inalienable rights; that among these are life, liberty, and the pursuit of happiness; that to secure these rights governments are instituted, deriving their just powers from the consent of the governed. Whenever any form of government becomes destructive of these ends, it is the right of those who suffer from it to refuse allegiance to it, and to insist upon the institution of a new government, laying its foundation on such principles, and organizing its powers in such form, as to them shall seem most likely to effect their safety and happiness. Prudence, indeed, will dictate that governments long established should not be changed for light and transient causes; and accordingly all experience hath shown that mankind are more disposed to suffer, while evils are sufferable, than to right themselves by abolishing the forms to which they are accustomed. But when a long train of abuses and usurpations, pursuing invariably the same object, evinces a design to reduce them under absolute despotism, it is their duty to throw off such government, and to provide new guards for their future security. Such has been the patient sufferance of the women under this government, and such is now the necessity which constrains them to demand the equal station to which they are entitled. The history of mankind is a history of repeated injuries and usurpations on the part of man toward woman, having in direct object the establishment of an absolute tyranny over her. To prove this, let facts be submitted to a candid world.

He has never permitted her to exercise her inalienable right to the elective franchise.

He has compelled her to submit to laws, in the formation of which she had no voice.

He has withheld from her rights which are given to the most ignorant and degraded men – both natives and foreigners.

Having deprived her of this first right of a citizen, the elective franchise, thereby leaving her without representation in the halls of legislation, he has oppressed her on all sides.

He has made her, if married, in the eye of the law, civilly dead. He has taken from her all right in property, even to the wages she earns.

He has made her, morally, an irresponsible being, as she can commit many crimes with impunity, provided they be done in the presence of her husband.

In the covenant of marriage, she is compelled to promise obedience to her husband, he becoming, to all intents and purposes, her master – the law giving him power to deprive her of her liberty, and to administer chastisement.

He has so framed the laws of divorce, as to what shall be the proper causes, and in case of separation, to whom the guardianship of the children shall be given, as to be wholly regardless of the happiness of women – the law, in all cases, going upon a false supposition of the supremacy of man, and giving all power into his hands.

After depriving her of all rights as a married woman, if single, and the owner of property, he has taxed her to support a government which recognizes her only when her property can be made profitable to it.

He has monopolized nearly all the profitable employments, and from those she is permitted to follow, she receives but a scanty remuneration. He closes against her all the avenues to wealth and distinction which he considers most honourable to himself. As a teacher of theology, medicine, or law, she is not known.

He has denied her the facilities for obtaining a thorough education, all colleges being closed against her.

He allows her in Church, as well as State, but a subordinate position, claiming Apostolic authority for her exclusion from the ministry, and, with some exceptions, from any public participation in the affairs of the Church.

He has created a false public sentiment by giving to the world a different code of morals for men and women, by which moral delinquencies which exclude women from society, are not only tolerated, but deemed of little account in man.

He has usurped the prerogative of Jehovah himself, claiming it as his right to assign for her a sphere of action, when that belongs to her conscience and to her God.

He has endeavoured, in every way that he could, to destroy her confidence in her own powers, to lessen her self-respect and to make her willing to lead a dependent and abject life.

Now, in view of this entire disfranchisement of one-half the people of this country, their social and religious degradation, in view of the unjust laws above mentioned, and because women do feel themselves aggrieved, oppressed, and fraudulently deprived of their most sacred rights, we insist that they have immediate admission to all the rights and privileges which belong to them as citizens of the United States.

In entering upon the great work before us, we anticipate no small amount of misconception, misrepresentation, and ridicule; but we shall use every instrumentality within our power to effect our object. We shall employ agents, circulate tracts, petition the State and National legislatures, and endeavour to enlist the pulpit and the press in our behalf. We hope this Convention will be followed by a series of Conventions embracing every part of the country.

Whereas, the great precept of nature is conceded to be, that 'man shall pursue his own true and substantial happiness,' Blackstone in his Commentaries remarks that this law of Nature being coeval with mankind, and dictated by God himself, is of course superior in obligation to any other. It is binding over all the globe, in all countries and at all times; no human laws are of any validity if contrary to this, and such of them as are valid, derive all their force, and all their validity, and all their authority, mediately and immediately, from this original; therefore,

Resolved, That such laws as conflict, in any way with the true and substantial happiness of woman, are contrary to the great precept of nature and of no validity, for this is 'superior in obligation to any other.'

Resolved, That all laws which prevent woman from occupying such a station in society as her conscience shall dictate, or which place her in a position inferior to that of man, are contrary to the great precept of nature, and therefore of no force or authority.

Resolved, That woman is man's equal, was intended to be so by the Creator, and the highest good of the race demands that she should be recognized as such.

Resolved, That the women of this country ought to be enlightened in regard to the laws under which they live, that they may no longer publish their degradation by declaring themselves satisfied with their present position, nor their ignorance, by asserting that they have all the rights they want.

Resolved, That inasmuch as man, while claiming for himself intellectual superiority, does accord to woman moral superiority, it is pre-eminently his duty to encourage her to speak and teach, as she has an opportunity, in all religious assemblies.

Resolved, That the same amount of virtue, delicacy, and refinement of behaviour that is required of woman in the social state, should also be required of man, and the same transgressions should be visited with equal severity on both man and woman.

Resolved, That the objection of indelicacy and impropriety, which is so often brought against woman when she addresses a public audience, comes with a very ill-grace from those who encourage, by their attendance, her appearance on the stage, in the concert. Or in feats of the circus.

Resolved, That woman has too long rested satisfied in the circumscribed limits which corrupt customs and a perverted application of the Scriptures have marked out for her, and that it is time she should move in the enlarged sphere which her great Creator has assigned her.

Resolved, That it is the duty of the women of this country to secure to themselves their sacred right to the elective franchise.

Resolved, That the equality of human rights results necessarily from the fact of the identity of the race in capabilities and responsibilities.

Resolved, therefore, That, being invested by the Creator with the same capabilities, and the same consciousness of responsibility for their exercise, it is demonstrably the right and duty of woman, equally with man, to promote every righteous cause by every righteous means; and especially in regard to the great subjects of morals and religion, it is self-evidently her right to participate with her brother in teaching them, both in private and in public, by writing and by speaking, by any instrumentalities proper to be used, and in any assemblies proper to be held; and this being a self-evident truth growing out of the divinely implanted principles of human nature, any custom or authority adverse to it, whether modern or wearing the hoary sanction of antiquity, is to be regarded as a self-evident falsehood, and at war with mankind.

Resolved, That the speedy success of our cause depends upon the zealous and untiring efforts of both men and women, for the overthrow of the monopoly of the pulpit, and for the securing to women an equal participation with men in the various trades, professions, and commerce.

Elizabeth Cady Stanton, Susan B. Anthony and Matilda J. Gage, eds, 'Declaration of Sentiments', in *History of Woman Suffrage*, Rochester, NY, 1881, vol. I, pp. 67–94

ST THÉRÈSE OF LISIEUX

Thérèse restates from her own reading and experience the great truth that God loves the poor in spirit, the simple of heart, and the children of light.

God loves simplicity

What is simpler and purer than a dewdrop? It is not formed by the *clouds*, because dew falls on the flowers when the vault of heaven is filled with stars. Rain is not to be compared with it, for it surpasses the rain in freshness and beauty. Dew exists only by night; the sun, darting its warm rays upon it, distils the lovely pearls sparkling on the tip of the blades of grass in the meadow, and the dew changes into a light vapour. Céline is a drop of dew, not formed by the clouds but come down from the loveliness of heaven, her Homeland. During the *night* of life it is its mission to be hid in the heart of the *Flower of the Fields*; no human eye can find it, only the cup that holds the tiny dewdrop can know its freshness. . . .

Our Beloved has no need of our fine thoughts – it is not intellect or talents that Jesus has come upon earth to seek. He became the Flower of the fields solely to show us how he loves simplicity. The *Lily in the valley* does not aspire to more than a drop of dew. That is why he created one, called Céline! During the night of this life, she is to remain hid from every human eye, but . . . the moment he appears in his glory . . . the divine Luminary, looking upon his dewdrop, will draw it upward to him and it will ascend like a light vapour and go where it may abide for eternity in the bosom of the glowing furnace of uncreated Love, forever united with him. . . . Jesus . . . wants his dewdrops not even to be aware of themselves . . . only he regards them; and they, not realizing their value, think of themselves below other creatures . . . and that is what the *Lily of the valley* desires.

Thérèse of Lisieux, *Oeuvres Complètes*, Paris, 2001, p. 461; *Collected Letters*, tr. F. Sheed, London and New York, 1949, pp. 163–5; also in Felicity Leng, *Smiles of God: The Flowers of St Thérèse of Lisieux*, London, 2003, p.112

EVELYN UNDERHILL

At an early stage in her writing life, Evelyn Underhill stressed the unpredictability of spiritual perception in a reply to a correspondent impressed by the 'spiritualist' novel The Grey World.

A sudden, strange light

As you say the finding of reality is the one thing that matters, and that always has mattered, though it has been called by many different names. You say in one place that the more urgent the want of reality grows, the less you see how to effect it. Now this state of spiritual unrest can never bring you to a state of vision of which the essential is peace. And struggling to see does not help one see. The light comes when it does come, rather suddenly and strangely, I think. It is just like falling in love; a thing that never happens to those who are always trying to do it. . . .

When once it has happened to you to perceive that beauty is the outward and visible sign of the greatest of sacraments, I don't think you can ever again get hopelessly entangled by its merely visible side. The real difficulty seems to me to come from the squalor and ugliness with which man seems to overlay the world in which he lives.

M. Cropper, *Life of Evelyn Underhill*, London, 1958, p. 25

CHARLOTTE YONGE

Yonge's didacticism sometimes has only a period charm, as when the hero of The Heir of Redclyffe, *a young man of 'almost deliquescent piety', refuses to take his horse to Oxford 'lest the temptations of the University city should prove too much for the morals of his groom'. But nearly all Yonge's novels contain many examples of her considerable ability to describe with pace and variety a realistic scene from everyday middle-class life that not only exemplifies the great Victorian theme of seeking out one's Christian duty so that one may execute it, but symbolizes some aspect of a conscience steering warily along the via media between, say, permissible pleasure and vanity, or between true achievement and popular success. This scene from* The Daisy Chain *is an instance of Yonge's skill in this respect.*

Not all is vanity

'You see, we have the prestige of better birth, and better education, as well as of having the chief property in the town, and of being the largest subscribers . . . ,' said Flora; 'so that everything conspires to render us leaders, and our age alone prevented us from assuming our post sooner'.

They were at home by this time, and, entering the hall, perceived that the whole party were on the lawn. The consolation of the children for the departure of Hector and Tom, was a bowl of soap-suds and some tobacco-pipes, and they had collected in the house to admire and assist; even Margaret's couch being drawn close to the window.

Bubbles are one of the most fascinating sports. There is the soft foamy mass, like driven snow or like whipped cream. Blanche bends down to blow 'a honeycomb', holding the bowl of the pipe in the water; at her gurgling blasts there slowly heaves upwards the pile of larger, clearer bubbles, each reflecting the whole scene, and sparkling with rainbow tints, until Aubrey ruthlessly dashes all into fragments with his hand, and Mary pronounces it stiff enough, and presents a pipe to little Daisy, who, drawing the liquid into her mouth, throws it away with a grimace, and declares that she does not like bubbles! But Aubrey stands with swelled cheeks, gravely puffing at the sealing-waxed extremity. Out pours a confused assemblage of froth, but the glassy globe slowly expands, the little branching veins, flowing down on either side, bearing an enlarging miniature of the sky, the clouds, the tulip-tree. Aubrey pauses to exclaim! But where is it? Try again! A proud bubble, as Mary calls it, a peacock in blended pink and green, is this transparent sphere, reflecting and embellishing house, wall, and shrubs! It is too beautiful! It is gone! Mary undertakes to give a lesson, and blows deliberately without the slightest result. Again! She waves her disengaged hand in silent exultation as the airy balls detach themselves, and float off on the summer breeze, with a tardy, graceful, uncertain motion. Daisy rushes after them, catches at them, and looks at her empty fingers with a puzzled 'All gone!' as plainly expressed by Toby, who snaps at them, and shakes his head with offended dignity at the shock of his meeting teeth, while the kitten frisks after them, striking at them with her paw, amazed at meeting vacancy.

Even the grave Norman is drawn in. He agrees with Mary that bubbles used to fly over the wall, and that one once went into Mrs Richardson's garret window, when her housemaid tried to catch it with a pair of tongs, and then ran down-stairs screaming that there was a ghost in her room; but that was in Harry's time, the heroic age of the May nursery.

He accepts a pipe, and his greater height raises it into a favourable current of air – the glistening balloon sails off. It flies, it soars; no, it is coming down! The children shout at it as if to drive it up, but it wilfully descends – they rush beneath, they try to waft it on high with their breath – there is a collision between Mary and Blanche – Aubrey perceives a taste of soapy water – the bubble is no more – it has vanished in his open mouth!

Papa himself has taken a pipe, and the little ones are mounted on chairs, to be on a level with their tall elders. A painted globe is swimming along, hesitating at first, but the dancing motion is tending upwards, the rainbow tints glisten in the sunlight – all rush to assist it; if breath of the lips can uphold it, it should rise, indeed! Up! Above the wall! Over Mrs Richardson's elm, over the topmost branch – hurrah! Out of sight! Margaret adds her voice to the acclamations. Beat that if you can, Mary! That doubtful wind keeps yours suspended in a graceful minuet; its pace is accelerated – but earthwards! It has committed self-destruction by running foul of a rose-bush. A general blank! . . .

'Hurrah for Blanche! Well done, white Mayflower, there!' said the Doctor, 'that is what I meant. See the applause gained by a proud bubble that flies! Don't we all bow down to it, and waft it up with the whole force of our lungs, air as it is; and when it fairly goes out of sight, is there any exhilaration or applause that surpasses ours?'

'The whole world being bent on making painted bubbles fly over the house,' said Norman, far more thoughtfully than his father. 'It is a fair pattern of life and fame.'

Charlotte Yonge, *The Daisy Chain*, London, 1879, part II, ch. V, pp. 379–81

Suffering and Persecution

AGNES BEAUMONT

Agnes Beaumont, one in a long line of religious women interro-
gated and threatened for their nonconforming beliefs, affirms
her innocence, rejects the kind of false accusation (by an envi-
ous suitor) of collusion with well-known dissidents or heretics in
criminal acts met with in so many countries over the centuries,
and looks for assurance to the one Source of her inward convic-
tion. The direct style reflects her awareness that she is one with
the disciples and early martyrs.

The presence of God

Though, as I said, I see my life lie at stake; for I did not know
how far God might suffer Him and the devil to go. And this also
troubled me, that if I had suffered another as innocent as I must
have suffered too; for Mr. Feery said that I made a hand of my
father, and John Bunyan gave me counsel to poison him when he
carried me behind him to Gamgy; that then we did consent to do
it. Nay, as I remember, it was said that Mr. Bunyan gave me stuff
to do it with. But the Lord knew to the contrary, that neither he
nor I was guilty of that wickedness in thought, word, nor deed.
But yet not withstanding I knew myself clear, yet I must tell you, I
see myself surrounded with strait and trouble; and carnal reasoning got in. Thought I, 'Suppose God should suffer my enemies to
prevail, to take away my life; how shall I endure burning?' Oh,
this made my heart ache at a great rate; though, blessed be God,

my heart did not accuse me, in thought, word, nor deed. But the thoughts of burning would sometimes shake me all to pieces; and sometimes I should think of that Scripture that would so often run in my mind before my father died, 'When thou goest through fire, I will be with thee; and through the waters, they shall not over flow thee'. And then I should think thus, 'Lord, thou knowest I am innocent; therefore if it shall please thee to suffer them to take away my life, yet surely thou wilt be with me. Thou hast been with me in all my straits, and I hope thou will not leave me now in the greatest of all'. And arguing thus from the experience of God's goodness to me in times of trial, at last I was made to believe that, if I did burn at a stake, the Lord would give me his presence. So I was made, in a solemn manner I hope, to resign myself up to God, to be at his disposing, for life or death.

The Narrative of the Persecution of Agnes Beaumont: A Diary, ed. G. B. Harrison, London, n.d., pp. 71–3

ST CATHERINE OF GENOA

Catherine of Genoa describes the fine movements of conscience in typically physical terms, and exemplifies her idea that the journey of suffering that leads to God begins in this life with a struggle between love for God and love of self.

A profound aspiration

Son, I have had a certain prick of conscience, of which I will tell you. The other day, when you told me that I might possibly remain dead some day during one of those giddiness's, there seemed to arise in me, at that moment, a feeling of joy, a profound aspiration which said: 'O, if that hour would only come!' And then this feeling suddenly ceased. Now I declare to you, that I do not wish that in this matter there should be any glimpse of a desire of my own for earth or heaven, or for any other created thing; but that I wish to leave all things to the disposition of God. He answered, that there was no occasion for her to have a prick of conscience, because, although joy had awaked in her mind, and a sudden exclamation had occurred there, at the mention of the word 'death', yet that nothing of this had proceeded from the will, nor had it been endorsed by the reason; but that it had proceeded solely from the instinct of the pleasure-loving soul, which ever, according to its nature, tends to such an end. And how the proof that this was a correct account, lay in this, that her prick of conscience had not really penetrated to the depths of her heart, but had remained on the surface, at the same slight depth at which the movement of joy had remained. And she confessed that the matter really stood thus, and remained satisfied.

Friedrich von Hügel, *The Mystical Element of Religion as Studied in Saint Catherine of Genoa and Her Friends*, vol. I, London, 1908, p. 192

JULIAN OF NORWICH

Julian of Norwich produces a variation on one of the great images of Christian thought when she offers her own interpretation of the notion of the universe suffering in sympathy with the passion and death of its Saviour.

A great oneing

I saw a great oneing between Christ and us because when he was in pain we were in pain. All creatures of God's creation that can suffer pain suffered with him. The sky and the earth failed at the time of Christ's dying because he too was part of nature.

Matthew Fox, *Original Blessing*, Santa Fe, 1983, p. 146

FLORENCE NIGHTINGALE

Before she became a public figure and national heroine, Florence Nightingale was well aware of the sinful waste of women's abilities in her own times. She remarked in her 1847–9 notebook:

Private martyrs

There are private martyrs as well as burnt or drowned ones. Society . . . does not know them; and the family cannot, because our position to one another in our families is . . . like that of the moon to the earth. The moon revolves around her, moves with her, never leaves her. Yet the earth never sees but one side of her; the other side remains for ever unknown.

Sir Edward Cook, *The Life of Florence Nightingale*, vol. I, New York, 1942, p. 59

ST EDITH STEIN

Edith Stein, who was forced to undergo an appalling fate herself even before she was gassed in Auschwitz, knew that no lessons would be learnt from the disaster of World War I unless those who had been through it worked together for positive ends: 'The nations of Europe fought to the death in the World War and suffered one and the same catastrophe. The harsh reality of suffering enabled them all to understand that they could progress only if they did so together.' Seeking to put this common pain in an eternal context, she could only conclude that there was a human vocation to suffer with Christ.

Children of grace

Only children of grace can in fact be bearers of Christ's cross. Only in union with the divine Head does human suffering take on expiatory power. To suffer and to be happy although suffering, to have one's feet on the earth, to walk on the dirty and rough paths of this earth and yet to be enthroned with Christ at the Father's right hand, to laugh and cry with the children of this world and ceaselessly sing the praises of God with the choirs of angels – this is the life of the Christian until the morning of eternity breaks forth.

The Hidden Life: Essays, Meditations, Spiritual Texts, in *Collected Works of Edith Stein*, Washington, DC, 1987ff., vol. IV, p. 93; also in Sarah Borden, *Edith Stein*, London, 2003, p. 130

SIMONE WEIL

Simone Weil's idea of 'waiting in patience' for God in an atheistic age had much in common with other essentially Christian thinkers of her times, such as Dietrich Bonhoeffer, but was also coloured by her reading of Hindu religion.

Identification

One should identify oneself with the universe itself. Everything that is less than the universe is subjected to suffering.

Simone Weil, *Notebooks*; cited by Susan Griffin, *Woman and Nature: The Roaring Inside Her*, New York, 1978, p. 219

Compassion and Forgiveness

৯৮

ELIZABETH FRY

Elizabeth Fry's God-given compassion that fed the intensity of her social conscience is powerfully evident in her preaching.

What owest thou unto thy Lord?

Are there not many here present whose desires are raised up to the living God, and to his kingdom of everlasting rest and peace, who are ready to adopt this language, 'Oh Lord revive thy work in the midst of the years' and are there not among you some of the bowed down, of the broken hearted, some who have many trials of faith and of patience, some of those conflicts which are much hidden from the eye of man? Oh! my friends, remember that we have to deal with a compassionate Father, who pitieth his children, who knoweth our frame, who remembereth that we are dust, who seeth us not as man seeth, who judgeth us not according to appearance, but according to the heart. Oh! my friends, whatever be the trials of your faith and of your patience, I sympathize with you; I desire that you may be upheld, that you may be strengthened, that you may find the grace of your Lord to be sufficient for you; and if we poor frail, feeble, unworthy mortals can feel as we do at seasons one for another, oh, what consolation is it to remember, that he who is infinite in mercy, infinite in love, and infinite in power also feels for us; we have a High Priest who is touched with the sense of our infirmities. Oh, my friends, however many of you may be cast down for a season, however you may not know any peace, oh, trust in the Lord and stay yourselves on your God, for his tender mercies are over all his works. Oh, remember, that the very hairs of your head are all numbered; remember that not a sparrow falls to the ground without him, and you are of much more value than many sparrows. Were not these expressions made use of by our blessed Lord for the encouragement of his poor little tender ones, those who are brought very low before him? How consoling is it to remember that there is no desire however feeble after himself but he regards it, he is willing to strengthen it, and it rises before him even as a pure and acceptable sacrifice, therefore ye humble, broken-hearted, contrite, and afflicted ones, lift up your hearts and put your trust in him who suffered for you, who was despised and rejected of men, a man of sorrows and acquainted with grief. Oh, how he did bear our sorrows; what an encouragement is it for us to remember this in all our tribulations, of whatever nature they may be, that the Lord can make all our trials, as well as all our blessings, work together for our good. Oh, may the language of our hearts increasingly be unto the Lord, 'that which I know not, teach thou me; if I have done iniquity, I will do so no more'. Oh, may we be strengthened to walk closer to God, to cleave very close unto him in spirit, to follow the Lamb our Saviour whithersoever he leadeth us, to make it the first business of our lives to be conformed to his will and to live to his glory, whether we pass through heights or depths, whether prosperity or adversity be our portion, though our years pass away as a tale that is told, the blessings of the Most High will rest upon us, and through his unbounded love, and through his unmerited mercy in Christ Jesus, we may indeed humbly trust that when this passing scene is closed to our view, an entrance will be granted unto us, even abundantly ministered unto us, into the everlasting kingdom of our Lord and Saviour Jesus Christ.

Indeed it is well for us, my friends, to enquire, 'What owest thou unto thy Lord?' Ah, dear friends, is it not well for us to do this when we reflect on what he hath done for us, even He who was wounded for our transgressions, who was bruised for our iniquities; the chastisement of our peace, we may remember, was on him, and by his stripes we are healed. It is well for us to remember what he hath been from time to time doing for us in the visitations of his love unto our souls; how often have the proofs of his love been extended towards us to gather us and keep us within his sacred enclosure, even the revelation of the will of God through Jesus Christ our Lord, our hope of glory. Oh, then seeing, my brethren and sisters, that the work is a progressive one, the enquiry arose in the secret of my heart, is our salvation nearer than when we first believe? What do we owe unto the Lord? what can we rightly perform that he may be pleased to receive at our hands? and the language of the Psalmist came before the view of my mind with renewed instruction, whilst I have been led to believe that he, the Lord Almighty who dwelleth on high, is calling upon us to go forward, to look not behind, to tarry not in the plain: 'Who shall ascend unto the hill of the Lord, and who shall stand in his holy place? he that hath clean hands and a pure heart, who hath not lifted his soul unto vanity, nor sworn deceitfully; he shall receive the blessing from the Lord, and righteousness from the God of his salvation.'

A sermon delivered by Elizabeth Fry, date and place unknown, in: *Sermons Preached by Members of the Society of Friends*, London, 1832, pp. 25–8

LUCRETIA MOTT

Lucretia Mott's address is a powerful example of women's preaching when skill in presentation and structure accompanied strengh of conviction, about, for instance, the inherent rectitude of the anti-slavery cause, war for war's sake, or the subjection of women.

Righteousness exalteth a nation

'Righteousness exalteth a nation, but sin is a reproach to any people.'

The Scriptures derive advantage from the fact that we find therein so uniform a testimony to the right; that is, among those who are not bound by sect, or devoted to forms and ceremonies. 'Your new moons and appointed feasts, your Sabbaths, even the solemn meeting,' were classed as abominations, and for the reason that they executed not judgment and justice and mercy in the land. The injunction was 'Learn to do well; seek judgment, relieve the oppressed, judge the fatherless, plead for the widow.' If they put away their iniquities, and did that which was right, then they should find acceptance. This is the testimony from age to age, as we find it recorded; and in time we should discriminate between those scriptures that conflict with righteous principles, and such as emanate from a spiritual understanding of the requirements of truth. . . . The more we appeal to the inner consciousness and perception of truth as received intuition, by divine instinct in the soul, and not through forms, ceremonies, and dogmas, the more will there be amendment in the conduct of life. Our appeals would be more effectual, were religion stripped of the dark theologies that encumber it, and its operations will prove more availing when presented to the hearers and to the thinkers free from the gloomy dogmas of sects.

The true gospel is not identical with any scheme or theological plan of salvation, however plausibly such a scheme may be drawn from isolated passages of Scripture, ingeniously woven; it is through the intelligence of the age, the progress of civilization, and individual thinking, that the right of judgment has been so far attained, that there is great daring of thought, of belief and expression, and much shortening of the creeds. A great deal that was demoralizing in its tendency has been separated from them. Still, what remains is so tenaciously held as the only touchstone of religious character, that there is a proportionate lessening of the effect of sound morals, and a lowering of the true standard. While we should feel a largeness of heart towards all religious denominations, at the same time, if we are true to God and the divine principle of his blessed Son, we must ever hold up the blessing to the merciful, the pure, the upright; regarding honesty, goodness, every-day works of usefulness and love, as paramount to all the peace and enjoyment that would follow an adherence to any of the abstract propositions of faith, that are held as the touchstone of sound Christianity. We must be as Jesus was, a non-conformist. That peace which 'passeth understanding' comes from obedience to truth, not to sect, for great hardness of heart often proceeds from this; it leads not to love, but to persecution and bitterness. Unless the faith of the sectarian is worked by a love, not of its own sect merely, but such as can go out beyond its own inclosure, to gather in the outcast and the oppressed, it is not efficient conversion. The apostle Paul believed he was acting in good conscience when he was a great persecutor, and no doubt many of the persecutors that perform their vile acts towards men, believe they are doing God's service; their acts are wicked nevertheless. Many go so far as to say that if a man does what he believes to be right, he is exempt from guilt. This is a mistake. We have far too much charity for any wrong-doer. What is wrong in itself, is wrong for anyone to do. The truth must be spoken, and the dark conscience enlightened.

Many persons have become so inured to slavery as not to discern its sinfulness. It has been said that 'no one in his inmost heart ever believed slavery to be right'. We know there is this instinct in man, else it would never have been proclaimed that all men are born equal, and endowed by their Creator with the inalienable right to life, liberty, and the pursuit of happiness. Many have so seared their minds that the light of the glorious gospel, which is the image of God, does not and cannot shine in upon them. Hence it is that in this day there should be an earnestness in advocating right doing. The people should be so enlightened as to distinguish between mere creeds and forms, and practical goodness.

It is irrational to deny the sinfulness of slavery . . . requirements of truth are the same in all ages, – to do right, to give freedom to the oppressed, the wronged, and the suffering. Those who have appealed in behalf of these, have not appealed in vain. Progress attends the work; but nothing can be effected by sitting still, and keeping aloof from the arena of activity; it is by labour, by many crosses, many sacrifices, – brother giving up brother unto death, and even submitting to martyrdom, – that beneficent results are accomplished. And what do we ask now? That slavery shall be held up in every congregation, and before all sects, as a greater sin than erroneous thinking; a greater sin than Sabbath breaking. If any of you are seen on Sabbath day with your thimble on, performing some piece of needlework, the feelings of your neighbours are shocked on beholding the sight; and yet these very people may be indifferent to great sins, regarding them with comparative unconcern, and even complacency. This is what I mean in saying that the standard of religious observances is placed higher than the standard of goodness, of uprightness, and of human freedom. To some, the sin of slaveholding is not so horrifying as certain deviations from established observances. While sticklers for these gather together and exhibit great marks of piety, in some instances they are guilty of small acts of unkindness, of meanness and oppression towards their neighbours. It is not enough to be generous, and give alms; the enlarged soul, the true philanthropist, is compelled by Christian principle to look beyond bestowing the scanty pittance to the mere beggar of the day, to the duty of considering the causes and sources of poverty. We must consider how much we have done towards causing it.

The feeling of opposition to war, that has been growing in the minds of men, is not confined to the Society of Friends; people of various denominations have examined this subject, and presented it in its true light. Faith in the efficacy of moral influences has increased, and the possibility of settling disputes without recourse to arms is being regarded more and more favourably. Still, the spirit of war exists, and it is surprising that those who look up to the Son and adore his sacred name should forget that the anthem of his advent upon the earth was 'Peace on earth, and good will to men.' . . .

The efforts that are making for the elevation of woman, the enlargement of her mind, the cultivation of her reasoning powers, and various ameliorating influences are preparing her to occupy a higher position than she has hitherto filled. She must come to judge within herself what is right, and absolve herself from that sectarian rule which sets a limit to the divinity within her. Whatever is a barrier to the development of her inherent, God-given powers, and to the improvement of her standing and character, whether it be ecclesiastical law or civil law, must be met and opposed. It is of more moment that she should be true and faithful to herself than to her sect.

A sermon delivered by Lucretia Mott at Bristol, PA, 1860, in Anna Davis Hallowell, ed., *James and Lucretia Mott: Life and Letters*, Boston, 1896

CORRIE TEN BOOM

In June 1945, after her release from prison at the end of the war, and after the liberation of the Netherlands, Corrie ten Boom felt the need to write one final letter to the person who had originally revealed to the Germans and collaborationist Dutch authorities her family's and Christian group's work in hiding Jews.

Dear Sir,

Today I heard that most probably you are the one who betrayed me. I went through ten months of concentration camp. My father died after nine days of imprisonment. My sister died in prison, too.

The harm you planned was turned into good for me by God. I am nearer to him. A severe punishment is awaiting you. I have prayed for you, that the Lord may accept you if you repent. Think that the Lord Jesus on the cross also took your sins upon himself. If you accept this and want to be his child, you are saved for eternity.

I have forgiven you everything. God will also forgive you everything, if you ask him. He loves you and he himself sent his son to earth to reconcile your sins, which meant to suffer the punishment for you and me. You, on your part, have to give an answer to this. If he says: 'Come unto me, give me your heart,' then your answer must be: 'Yes, Lord, I come, make me your child.' If it is difficult for you to pray, then ask if God will give you his Spirit, who works the faith in your heart.

Never doubt the Lord Jesus' love. He is standing with his arms spread out to receive you.

I hope that the path which you will now take may work for your eternal salvation.

Corrie ten Boom, *Prison Letters*, London, 1975, pp. 89–90

Imprisonment and Death

⁂

ANNE ASKEW

The examinations of Anne Askew

Under interrogation for her beliefs, Askew does not apologize for her lowly status, but answers her accusers with the folk wit and sacred cheek traditionally found in the acts of certain martyrs of the early Church and, notably, in the examinations of St Joan of Arc. This is particularly obvious when Anne states her concept of the key notion of transubstantiation, still professed by the Henrician Church. In her Examinations *Anne Askew takes for granted her right as a woman to discuss theological niceties usually expounded by male theologians and contenders, such as the Real Presence of Christ in the sacrament, which for her brand of Protestantism depended on the spiritual state of the minister and congregation. For Catholics, the consecrated bread would be Christ's Body, even if nibbled by a mouse.*

They said to me there that I was a heretic, and condemned by the law if I would stand in my opinion. I answered that I was no heretic, neither yet deserved I any death by the law of God. But as concerning the faith which I uttered and wrote to the council, I would not, I said, deny it, because I knew it true. Then they would needs know if I would deny the sacrament to be Christ's body and blood. I said, 'Yea, for the same son of God that was born of the Virgin Mary, is now glorious in heaven, and will come again from thence at the latter day, like as he went up (Acts 1). And as for that you call your God, is but a piece of bread. For a more proof of thereof (mark it when you list) yet it lie in the box but three months, and it will be mould and so turn to nothing that is good. Whereupon I am persuaded that it cannot be good.'

The same sturdy refusal to bow to any supposed superiority of gender or office is apparent through her first examination:

First Christopher Dare examined me at Saddlers' Hall . . . and asked if I did not believe that the sacrament hanging over the altar was the very body of Christ really. Then I demanded this question of him: wherefore Saint Stephen was stoned to death. And he said he could not tell. Then I answered that no more would I assoil his vain question.

Secondly, he said that there was a woman which did testify that I should read how God was not in temples made with hands. Then I showed him the seventh and the seventeenth chapters of the Acts of the Apostles, what Stephen and Paul had said therein. Whereupon he asked me how I took those sentences. I answered that I would not throw pearls among swine, for acorns were good enough.

Thirdly, he asked me wherefore I said that I had rather to read five lines in the Bible, than to hear five masses in the temple. I confessed that I said no less. Not for the dispraise of either the Epistle or Gospel, but because the one did greatly edify me, and the other nothing at all. As Saint Paul witnesses in the 14th chapter of his first Epistle to the Corinthians, where as he says: 'If the trumpet gives an uncertain sound, who will prepare himself to the battle?'

Fourthly, he laid unto my charge that I should say: 'If an ill priest ministered, it was the Devil and not God.' My answer was that I never spoke any such thing. But this was my saying: 'That whatsoever he were who ministered unto me, his ill conditions could not hurt my faith, but in spirit I received nevertheless the body and blood of Christ.' Fifthly, he asked me concerning confession. I answered him my meaning, which was as Saint James says, that every man ought to acknowledge his faults to another, and the one to pray for the other.

Sixthly, he asked me what I said to the king's book. And I answered him that I could say nothing to it, because I never saw it.

Seventhly, he asked me if I had the spirit of God in me. I answered if I had not, I was but reprobate or cast away. Then he said he had sent for a priest to examine me, which was there at hand. The priest asked me what I said to the sacrament of the altar. And required much to know therein my meaning. But I desired him again to hold me excused concerning that matter. None other answer would I make him, because I perceived him a papist.

Eighthly, he asked me if I did not think that private masses did help souls departed. And I said it was great idolatry to believe more in them than in the death which Christ died for us. Then they had me thence unto my Lord Mayor and he examined me, as they had before, and I answered him directly in all things as I answered the questions before. Besides this my Lord Mayor laid one thing unto my charge which was never spoken of me but of them. And that was whether a mouse eating the host received God or no. This question did I never ask, but indeed they asked it of me, whereunto I made them no answer but smiled. Then the Bishop's Chancellor rebuked me and said that I was much to blame for uttering the Scriptures. For Saint Paul (he said) forbade women to speak or to talk of the word of God. I answered him that I knew Paul's meaning as well as he, which is, 1 Corinthians 14, that a woman ought not to speak in the congregation by the way of teaching. And then I asked him how many women he had seen go into the pulpit and preach? He said he never saw none. Then I said, he ought to find no fault in poor women, except they had offended the law. Then my Lord Mayor commanded me to ward. I asked him if sureties would not serve me, and he made me short answer, that he would take none.

Then was I had to the Counter, and there remained 11 days, no friend admitted to speak with me. But in the meantime there was a priest sent to me who said that he was commanded of the Bishop to examine me, and to give me good counsel, which he did not. But first he asked me for what cause I was put in the Counter.

And I told him I could not tell. Then he said it was great pity that I should be there without cause, and concluded that he was very sorry for me.

Secondly, he said it was told him that I should deny the sacrament of the altar. And I answered him again that what I had said, I had said. Thirdly, he asked me if I were shriven. I told him so that I might have one of these three, that is to say, Doctor Crome, Sir William, or Huntingdon, I was contented, because I knew them to be men of wisdom. 'As for you or any other I will not dispraise, because I know you not.'

Then he said, 'I would not have you think but that I or another that shall be brought you shall be as honest as they. For if we were not, you may be sure, the king would not suffer us to preach.' Then I answered by the saying of Solomon, 'By communing with the wise, I may learn wisdom: But by talking with a fool, I shall take scathe' (Proverbs 1).

Fourthly, he asked me if the host should fall, and a beast did eat it, whether the beast did receive God or no. I answered, 'Seeing you have taken the pain to ask this question I desire you also to assoil it yourself. For I will not do it, because I perceive you come to tempt me.' And he said it was against the order of schools that he who asked the question should answer it. I told him I was but a woman and knew not the course of schools. Fifthly, he asked me if I intended to receive the sacrament at Easter or no. I answered that else I were no Christian woman, and there I did rejoice, that the time was so near at hand. And then he departed thence with many fair words. . . .

In the meanwhile he commanded his archdeacon to common with me, who said unto me, 'Mistress, wherefore are you accused and thus troubled here before the Bishop?' To whom I answered again and said, 'Sir, ask, I pray you, my accusers, for I know not as yet.' Then took he my book out of my hand and said, 'Such books as this hath brought you to the trouble you are in. Beware,' says he, 'beware, for he that made this book and was the author thereof was an heretic, I warrant you, and burnt in Smithfield.' Then I asked him if he were certain and sure that it was true that he had spoken. And he said he knew well the book was of

John Frith's making. Then I asked him if he were not ashamed for to judge of the book before he saw it within or yet knew the truth thereof. I said also that such unadvised and hasty judgment is token apparent of a very slender wit. Then I opened the book and showed it to him. He said he thought it had been another, for he could find no fault therein. Then I desired him no more to be so unadvisedly rash and swift in judgment, till he thoroughly knew the truth, and so he departed from me.

The Account of the Sufferings of Anne Askew . . . written by herself, London, 1849, pp. 38, 79–80

MARGIAD EVANS

Margiad Evans wrote a poem which she entitled 'Traveller's Joy' in which she proposed various answers to anyone who might ask where she had gone, including 'she is travelling in the grave' and 'the roots are million that return', and explained her understanding of death.

Absence is presence altered

The clue to this poem, every word of which meant much to me and was as exact as I could make it, was the word roots, 'the roots are million that return'. The poem is a statement of my conviction that my being and all natural life were in substance and spirit, one, and that in one form or another, life lives on. It is not a particular requiem like some which followed it. This unity, or Oneness, experienced by . . . many lunatics, by mystics, with the Universe I believe to be only the first state of God's appearance to the sufferer. All mystics begin as Nature mystics. Some, like Jefferies and Lawrence, stay there, but more go on, having begun, if they live.

Margiad Evans, *A Ray of Darkness*, London, 1952, pp. 22–3

MARIE BASHKIRTSEFF

Marie Bashkirtseff's mixture of intimate gossipy tone and self-criticism, but also her analytical descriptions of the necessarily divided nature of a modern woman ('The woman writing and the one I describe are two separate beings'), represent a very up-to-date and skilled approach to dealing responsibly with an inescapable death-sentence while continuing to recognize the hopes and ambitions but also resentments of youth.

Illusion and reality

I spent some time in the Bon Marché store, which I like so much, like everything sharp and well-organized. We had guests to dinner and there was lots of laughter. I was laughing too, but in reality it was and is all much of a muchness . . . because I'm actually rather sad and desolate.

It's impossible! Death! What a vile, destructive, repellent and hateful word! Dying, good Lord! Dying! To have to die! Without leaving anything behind? Dying like a dog as so many hundreds of thousands of women have died whose names are scarcely legible on their gravestones? To have to die . . . like . . . But how crazy, how very crazy of me not to see the meaning of it: to realize what God wants! What does he want? Obviously he wants me to abandon everything else and devote myself to art! In five years' time I'll still be quite young, and perhaps even good-looking, beautiful even. . . . But what good will that be if I'm only mediocre as an artist, like so many others?

It wouldn't matter so much otherwise, but if you spend so much time dedicating your life to something, and then achieve nothing at all after all that effort, you have to ask: What can it possibly mean?

Isn't some kind of response to what you do essential? What can you achieve on your own without that? It's enough to make me hate and run down the whole world, my family and myself! Holy Mary, Mother of God, Lord Jesus Christ, God my God, help me!

But if you really want to be an artist you have to go to Italy!! Yes, to Rome.

Oh, but what about this great impenetrable stone wall that I just keep running up against and banging my head on every minute?

I shall have to stay here.

I sketched a portrait of the housemaid, Antoinette. She has a lovely face and great big shining blue eyes which are so extraordinarily gentle and innocent. Yes, I've got something of her, my sketch is on the right tracks, but to get it right you have to have studied art properly.

I start imagining that Rome is the only place where I could possibly live. . . .

Sad to say, you only begin to discover what you should really do when it's too late to do anything at all.

Painting makes me furious, because I know that I've got it in me to do marvellous things, but as far as studying is concerned, I'm worse than any little beginner in whom they've spotted some small talent and who is about to be sent off to school for the first time. Anyway I'm so angry about it all and about what I've lost and what I might have done that I start hoping that my entire family will be polished off once I'm dead, and even imagine them being sent to the guillotine.

Marie Bashkirtseff, *Journal*, Paris, 1887, entries for 7–18 August 1877

EMILY JANE BRONTË

Emily Brontë's poem of 2 January 1846 is an assertion of spiritual confidence produced by a passionate spirit steeped in the Authorized Version of the Bible, the Book of Common Prayer, *Shakespeare, Scott and the Border Ballads, aware of the inward effects as well as the outward presence of the noble yet threatening Yorkshire countryside, and battered yet not vanquished but strangely invigorated by inner turmoil. Charlotte said of Emily's poems: 'I thought them condensed and terse, vigorous and genuine. To my ear they also had a peculiar music – wild, melancholy*

and elevating.' She also remarked of Emily that 'out of a sullen
hollow in a livid hillside her mind could make an Eden', for Emily
rejected a conventional heaven and dreamed of an immortality
true to vital experience: 'I broke my heart with weeping to come
back to earth; and the angels were so angry that they flung me
out into the middle of the heath on the top of Wuthering Heights,
where I woke sobbing for joy' (Cathy in Wuthering Heights).

No coward soul is mine

No coward soul is mine
No trembler in the world's storm-troubled sphere
I see Heaven's glories shine
And Faith shines equal arming me from Fear

O God within my breast
Almighty ever-present Deity
Life, that in me hast rest
As I Undying Life, have power in Thee

Vain are the thousand creeds
That move men's hearts, unutterably vain,
Worthless as withered weeds
Or idlest froth amid the boundless main

To waken doubt in one
Holding so fast by thy infinity
So surely anchored on
The steadfast rock of Immortality

With wide-embracing love
Thy spirit animates eternal years
Pervades and broods above,
Changes, sustains, dissolves, creates and rears

Though Earth and moon were gone
And suns and universes ceased to be
And thou wert left alone
Every Existence would exist in thee

There is not room for Death
Nor atom that his might could render void
Since thou art Being and Breath
And what thou art may never be destroyed.

The Complete Poems of Emily Brontë, ed. C. W. Hatfield, New York,
1941, p. 244

EMILY DICKINSON

*Emily Dickinson's poem is an exquisite statement of the possible
inevitability yet infinite inappropriateness of oblivion.*

Because I could not stop . . .

Because I could not stop for Death –
He kindly stopped for me –
The Carriage held but just Ourselves –
And Immortality.

We slowly drove – He knew no haste
And I had put away
My labour and my leisure too,
For His Civility –

We passed the School, where Children strove
At Recess – in the Ring –
We passed the Fields of Gazing Grain –
We passed the Setting Sun –

Or rather – He passed Us –
The Dews drew quivering and chill –
For only Gossamer, my Gown –
My Tippet – only Tulle –

We paused before a House that seemed
A Swelling of the Ground –
The Roof was scarcely visible –
The Cornice – in the Ground –

Since then – 'tis Centuries – and yet
Feels shorter than the Day
I first surmised the Horses' Heads
Were toward Eternity –

c. 1863, publ. in *Poems by Emily Dickinson*, 1st series, eds M. L. Todd
and T. W. Higginson, Boston, 1890

ST EDITH STEIN

*Facing an unjust and savage death, Edith Stein makes acceptance
the keynote of her 'last will and testament'.*

Perfect submission

I joyfully accept in advance the death God has appointed for me,
in perfect submission to his most holy will. May the Lord accept
my life and death for the honour and glory of his name, for the
needs of his holy Church – especially for the preservation, sancti-
fication, and final perfecting of our holy Order, and in particular
for the Carmels of Cologne and Echt – for the Jewish people, that
the Lord may be received by his own and his Kingdom come in
glory, for the deliverance of Germany and peace throughout the
world, and finally, for all my relatives living and dead and all
whom God has given me: may none of them be lost.

Sarah Borden, *Edith Stein*, London, 2003, p. 136

CORRIE TEN BOOM

*In 1944, Corrie ten Boom, a devout evangelical Christian, had
spent several months in solitary confinement in Scheveningen
prison. She had learned of her father's death after his arrest for
hiding Jews from the Dutch police and the Gestapo. She now
writes to family and friends before deportation to a concentra-*

tion camp. She has no idea if she will survive whatever horrors are to come, but she tries to strengthen her family's faith.

Truly comforted

On the wall of my cell is written in English, 'Not lost, but gone before'. He will leave a great emptiness in my life. For the love and help I gave him, the Lord will surely provide many others. But what I received from him can never be replaced. What a privilege though that we could for so long so intensely enjoy him. For a few days I was upset. Now that has passed. During the last few days there was such a tension within me. I did not dare to think things through and when you are so alone it is difficult to get away from your thoughts. Now that is gone and I am thinking much about the future. I make plans and am experiencing much peace. How good the Saviour is to me! He not only bears my burdens. He carries me, too. . . .

Yes, Nollie, how difficult our path is, but the Saviour will give you a strong heart to go on at this time. I pray much for you. Please pray much for me. Bye, dear children and friends. God bless you all. . . .

Pray for guidance for me when I have to appear before the judge. I am not afraid. The Saviour never leaves me alone and he will not here either.

Much love, Corrie

Corrie ten Boom, *Prison Letters*, London, 1975, pp. 33–6

ST THÉRÈSE OF LISIEUX

Thérèse detested the frightening image of the grim reaper, with death shown as a skeleton with a scythe. She preferred the image of a benign God harvesting his souls as they ripened. She saw herself as a springtime flower, not only because she was born in the spring, but because she knew she had not long to live.

A spring flower

I am a spring flower gathered by the owner of the garden for his delight. We are all flowers planted on this earth and God gathers us up in his own good time, some earlier, others later. I am an ephemeral little creature, and I shall be the first to go.

Felicity Leng, *Smiles of God: The Flowers of St Thérèse of Lisieux*, London, 2003, p. 24

Joy and Peace

❧

ST CATHERINE OF SIENA

Catherine believed that the blood which Christ shed on the cross marks the beginning of the way we must take towards the God who re-creates us through love. On 1 April 1376, she had a vision of the divine purpose which she tried to explain to Brother Raimondo da Capua and other members of her 'family' who were already in Avignon (where, in her opinion, the Pope ought never to have been, for the residence of the papacy there contributed to division in the Church). They were awaiting her arrival.

Re-creation

My dearly beloved sons in Jesus Christ,

Love each other and be glad and rejoice! The summer is on its way. During the night of the first day of April, God was more open with his mysteries than ever before. He revealed his wonders so powerfully that I thought my soul was outside my body, and I was so overcome with joy that I can't possibly tell you how I felt. God described and explained in detail the mystery of the persecution presently suffered by holy Church, and of its future renewal and exaltation. He said that he allows present events to happen in order to restore the Church to her original state. He seemed to be saying: 'I allow this period of persecution in order to remove the brambles from my bride the Church, because she is quite surrounded by them. But I certainly don't allow people to plot the evil they have in mind. Do you understand what I am doing? I act as I did when I was in the world, and I made a whip of cords and drove from the Temple those who were selling and buying there, because I didn't want my Father's house to be turned into a thieves' den. You have to realize that, in the same way, I've turned certain people into a whip, and I'm using it to drive out the foul, greedy, avaricious dealers who are so puffed up with pride, and are selling and buying the Holy Spirit's graces and gifts.' This meant that he was using a whip of human persecution to drive them out. He was using suffering and persecution to liberate them from their appallingly disturbed way of life. . . .

I watched people, Christians and unbelievers alike, entering the side of the crucified Christ. In all my longing, and driven by love, I walked through that crowd of folk and joined them as they made their way into gentle Jesus Christ. I was accompanied by my father Saint Dominic, John the beloved, and all my children. Then he put the cross on my shoulder and the olive branch in my hand, to show (as he told me) that he wanted me to carry it to Christians and unbelievers alike. He said: 'Tell them: "I bring you news of great joy!" '

Then I rejoiced more than ever before. I was immersed in the divine Being, together with all the truly joyful, in unity and the joy of love. My soul rejoiced so utterly that I was no longer aware of the pain I had felt when I saw God offended. I said: 'O happy fault!'

Tender Jesus smiled at this, and said: 'Is sin happy now? Sin, which is nothingness? . . .'

I replied: 'I quite understand, dear Lord. I am well aware that sin is not worthy to be called happy or blessed, and is neither blessed nor happy. But the fruit that comes from sin is blessed and happy. I think that this is what Gregory meant: because of Adam's sin God gave us the Word, his only-begotten Son. And the Word gave us his blood. By surrendering his life, he gave us back grace with such glowing love. Therefore sin is happy not because it is sin, but because of the fruit and gift we receive because of that sin.' . . .

Accordingly, the sin committed by wicked Christians when

they persecute the bride of Christ gives rise to exaltation, light, and fragrant virtue in this bride. . . .

So be happy and rejoice! . . .

Carry on living in God's holy and tender love. Immerse your-selves in the blood of the crucified Christ. Do not hesitate for any reason. Be more resolute than ever before. Be happy, and rejoice in your pleasant labours.

Love, love, love each other!

Tender Jesus! Good Jesus! Loving Jesus! Jesus, Jesus!

S. Caterina da Siena, *La Verità dell'Amore* (selected letters), ed. G. Cavallini, Rome, 1978, p. 39

MARGIAD EVANS

Margiad Evans was aware how states of meditation and absence can disturb unsympathetic people.

Intervals of peace

I live by intervals of peace, where nothing is spoken but all is comprehended. Or would be if I weren't recalled. One is always being summoned. And people want answering. Unless one is in a state of perpetual reciprocity they imagine one to be either mad or angry. One looks out suddenly, and sees that, startled, they are waiting for a normal explanation of one's spiritual absence.

Margiad Evans, *Autobiography*, London, 1943, pp. 54–5

ST GERTRUDE OF HELFTA

For St Gertrude of Helfta the outcome of pious efforts could be a reciprocal process. She wrote her Legate of Divine Love *hoping that the ardour and serenity of her visions would help her readers, too, to glorify the graciousness of the Lord, but also that 'so sweet a fragrance 'would arise 'to thee from the golden censers of their hearts full of charity, as to make amends abundantly for all the defects of my ingratitude and negligence'. She insists on the importance of a holy life in assisting the salvation of as many other souls as possible. Its merits may even be applied to specific souls: 'Although the Church shares in each of the favours granted to each of the faithful, yet he who receives it has a greater benefit from it, and consequently anyone to whom he desires with a special affection to communicate it will also receive from it greater fruit and benefit.'*

No joys will be lacking

One day between Easter and Ascension I went into the garden before Prime, and, sitting down beside the pond, I began to consider what a pleasant place it was. I was charmed by the clear water and flowing streams, the fresh green of the surrounding trees, the birds flying so freely about, especially the doves. But most of all, I loved the quiet, hidden peace of this secluded retreat. I asked myself what more was needed to complete my happiness in a place that seemed to me so perfect, and I reflected that it was the presence of a friend, intimate, affectionate, wise and companionable, to share my solitude.

And then you, my God . . . made me understand that, if I were to pour back like water the stream of graces received from you . . . if, like a tree, growing in the exercise of virtue, I were to cover myself with the leaves and blossoms of good works; if, like the doves I were to spurn earth and soar heavenward; and if, with my senses set free from passions and worldly distractions, I were to occupy myself with you alone; then my heart would afford you a dwelling most suitably appointed from which no joys would be lacking.

Gertrude of Helfta, *The Herald of Divine Love*, tr. M. Winkworth, New York and Mahwah, NJ, 1993, Book II, p. 97

HILDEGARD OF BINGEN

Hildegard believed that a joyful response to another person is the soul remembering that God created it.

Holy breath of holiness

Holy breath of holiness and fire-brand of love!
Heart's joy flowing in sweet and fragrant virtue!
Clear glass in which we see God claim the lost
And bring home all those who are forgotten!
Saving way that knows no rock or barrier,
You are in the highest, lowest, deepest.
You join all that is, all who are.
Through you clouds billow and winds blow,
The earth bears fruit and springs burst forth,
Through you the world grows green with promise.
You lead us through the wastes of this world
And guide us through this life's darkness.
You breathe your wisdom into us
Filling us with joy and gladness.

Hildegard von Bingen, *Symphonia*, Gerlingen, 1995, p. 137

HROSWITHA OF GANDERSHEIM

Hroswitha exalts the divine aspect of human creativity and refers somewhat ironically (given her recognition at the imperial court, the quality of her work, and its production in an abbey whose abbess had a seat in the imperial diet) to the presumed inferiority of women's abilities.

Divine inspiration

In the midst of this I am torn between diverse impulses – joy and fear: indeed I feel joy deep in my heart that God, through whose grace I am what I am, is praised in me; yet I am afraid to seem

greater than I am – I have no doubt that both denying the spon-
taneously given gift of God and pretending to have received what
was not received are equally wrongful. . . .

Therefore, lest God's gift be annulled in me through my own
negligence, I have tried to tear some threads, or even shreds, of
cloth, snatching them from Philosophia's robe, to interweave
them with the present work, so that the wretchedness of my
ignorance be illumined by the intermingling of nobler stuff, and
that the bestower of genius be praised rightfully, and the more
copiously in that women's understanding is held to be more
retarded.

Peter Dronke, *Women Writers of the Middle Ages*, Cambridge, 1984,
pp. 74–5

JULIAN OF NORWICH

*Julian of Norwich describes God as a totally trustworthy, lov-
ing and benevolent father joyously delighting in his creation, and
becoming sad, not punitive, when his child lets him down.*

God never changes

I am sure that you cannot speak of anger in connection with God,
since Jesus is eternally concerned not only for the honour due to
him but for the good fortune of everyone who is to be counted
among the saved. Our Lord has set his power and justice against
the wickedness and sly tricks of the evil-minded who work against
God's will. I watched Jesus treat that wickedness with contempt
and reveal Satan's hollow impotence. He wants us to do just that.
When I saw all this, I laughed so resoundingly that everyone
around me started to laugh too, which pleased me greatly, and
I thought: I wish all my fellow-Christians could see exactly what
I have seen, then they would be able to laugh along with me. But I
didn't see Jesus laughing. It seemed to me that it was permissible
for us to laugh if we wanted to reassure ourselves and show our
holy joy that Satan has been foiled. Yet, when I saw Jesus scorn

that devilish evil, I was granted an inward vision of the truth, for Jesus' face didn't change. As I see it, one of the most praiseworthy things about God is that he is always the same. . . .

Contrition makes us clean, compassion prepares us, and true longing for God makes us worthy. It seems to me that these three things help souls to get to heaven. Every sinful soul has to take these medicines to be healed. Even when the soul has been healed, God perceives the wounds in it as marks of honour, rather than as wounds. The loving kindness of almighty God rewards us in heaven by . . . making sure that no one who arrives there will lose any of the benefits which his sufferings have earned for us. He considers sin in those whom he loves and who love him to be a sad thing and suffering, yet, because he loves us, not as worthy of blame . . . and thus shame is transformed into greater honour and joy.

Revelation 13 and 39, BNF MS 40 Fonds Anglais

DOROTHY L. SAYERS

Dorothy L. Sayers was a precisionist in the use of religious language, but might add a superb lyrical affirmation of a Christian truth to a corrective mini-sermon.

Joy and happiness

This tension between joy and the opposite of joy is, once again, something that is viewed with a certain distrust by an age committed to the pursuit of happiness. It can be readily pigeonholed as lack of adjustment or, in severe cases, as a psychosis. In very severe cases it may indeed a psychosis. But we must not disguise from ourselves that happiness is a gift of the heathen gods, whereas joy is a Christian duty. It was, I think, L. P. Jacks who pointed out that the word 'happiness' does not occur in the Gospels; the word 'joy', on the other hand, occurs frequently – and so does the name and image of Hell. The command is to rejoice: not to display a placid contentment or a stoic fortitude. 'Call no man happy until he is dead', said the Greek philosopher; and happiness, whether applied to a man's fortunes or his disposition, is the assessment of something extended in time along his whole career. But joy (except for those saints who live continually in the presence of God) is of its nature brief and almost instantaneous – it is an apprehension of the eternal moment. And, as such, it is the great invading adversary that can break open the gates of Hell.

Dorothy L. Sayers, *The Poetry of Search and the Poetry of Statement*, London, 1963, p. 84

Heaven and Eternity

ॐ

EMILY DICKINSON

Emily Dickinson's poem is a witty presentation of our innate refusal to accept dissolution.

Death is a Dialogue

Death is a Dialogue between
The Spirit and the Dust.
'Dissolve' says Death – The Spirit 'Sir
I have another Trust' –

Death doubts it – Argues from the Ground –
The Spirit turns away
Just laying off for evidence
An Overcoat of Clay.

c. 1864, publ. in *Poems by Emily Dickinson*, 1st series, eds M. L. Todd and T. W. Higginson, Boston, 1890

MARGIAD EVANS

Margiad Evans was able to represent eternity in almost Blake-like terms.

Pause and intensity

For the pause and the intensity within vision or revelation may occur anywhere in any surroundings. Whatever the circumstance, whether one is gardening, thinking of something or looking at a face, an animal or a leaf – that sight or state of mind is prolonged, it seems, although afterwards it will have been found to have fitted into clock time. The sight, however casual (of the leaf, say, as personally I have never experienced it looking at a person), is made to last; and the memory, like sharp scissors is meanwhile cutting round that shape which the consciousness will retain forever, or for as long as it itself lasts. So in that yogi-like experience of childhood, a breath was made to last, for me, for five minutes. Vision is something truly very simple – a breath, a leaf, but lengthened. Perhaps so is Eternity, just time made to last.

Margiad Evans, *A Ray of Darkness*, London, 1952, p. 176

JULIAN OF NORWICH

Ida Görres remarked that the 'shewings' of Julian of Norwich were 'flashes, not lamps', and that the 'seer needs the Church, for she alone provides the background against which his visions really make sense – instead of being simply isolated, crazy arabesques. The priest has to keep the whole, whatever is enduring, universal, catholic; to the prophet is committed the part, the renovation, what is new, as well as what must be renovated. His is the special task. But the second cannot be accomplished without the first. Only against the "common" outline of the whole, within its proportions, can the flash-lit details be understood. No point in enlarging a photograph of an eyelid, for instance, unless people know the face' (Broken Lights, London, 1964, p. 139).

Julian's visions are indeed flash-lit perceptions that illumine the whole that might otherwise seem mundane.

An invitation to a dinner-party

In my mind's eye I saw heaven and our Lord acting as the head of his house who had issued an invitation to a dinner-party for all his beloved servants and friends. I could see that Jesus did not take up any particular place in his house but presided over everything, making sure that the general atmosphere was one of joy and happiness. He was entirely at his ease and totally kind and civil, behaving so as to make his dear friends happy and comfortable for ever. The beauty of his holy face revealed the wonderful melody of his everlasting love. That glorious face fills heaven quite full of divine bliss and joy.

Revelation 14, BNF MS 40 Fonds Anglais

MARGERY KEMPE

Margery Kempe wrote a most joyous and homely account of the lay religious life.

Full merry in heaven

On a night, as this creature lay in her bed with her husband, she heard a sound of melody so sweet and delectable, that she thought she had been in Paradise, and therewith she started out of her bed and said:

'Alas, that ever I did sin! It is full merry in Heaven.'

This melody was so sweet that it surpassed all melody that ever might be heard in this world, without any comparison, and caused her, when she heard any mirth or melody afterwards, to have full plenteous and abundant tears of high devotion, with great sobbings and sighings after the bliss of Heaven, not dreading the shames and the spites of this wretched world. Ever after this inspiration, she had in her mind the mirth and the melody that was in Heaven, so much, that she could not well restrain herself from speaking thereof, for wherever she was in any company she would say oftentimes: 'It is full merry in Heaven.'

And they that knew her behaviour beforetime, and now heard her speaking so much of the bliss of Heaven, said to her:

'Why speak ye so of the mirth that is in Heaven? Ye know it not, and ye have not been there, any more than we.' And wroth with her, for she would not hear nor speak of worldly things as they did, and as she did beforetime.

The Book of Margery Kempe: A Modern Version, ed. W. Butler-Bowdon, London, 1936, p. 15

DOROTHY L. SAYERS

Dorothy L. Sayers could draw useful lessons from useless controversy, as in these astringent lines on heaven and hell.

Heaven and hell

I ought perhaps to say one word about the question which still sometimes bothers people, namely whether the Church officially teaches that the pains of Hell and the joys of Heaven are physical or 'only' spiritual. On this side of the Resurrection, the souls have no bodies: consequently the question has no meaning – or at most resolves itself into the rather academical one, discussed with some ingenuity by St Augustine, whether and how a spiritual being can suffer pain from a physical fire. After the Resurrection, there will be a body; but it will be, as St Paul says, 'a spiritual body', and since we do not know at all what it will be like, we cannot tell how it may be able to suffer or rejoice. The danger of saying explicitly, as some theologians have always said, that the pains and joys of spirits are wholly spiritual is that the sort of person who reads *The Freethinker* is then moved to say: 'Oh, merely figurative' – as though nothing were really real except the pleasure of sun-bathing and the pains of toothache. What is meant by the stress sometimes laid upon the physical aspect of both pain and joy is that it is real, and that it involves the whole personality.

Dorothy L. Sayers, *Introductory Papers on Dante*, New York, 1957, p. 57

ST THÉRÈSE OF LISIEUX

Thérèse's mother had asked her dying sister to run some errands for her when she entered heaven. Thérèse spoke and wrote in the same vein. She saw heaven not as an inaccessible place of inactivity, where she would bask in the glory of God, but as somewhere to continue her work on earth. She would be someone whom the living could call on and ask favours from. She in turn would send down her 'shower of roses'. A few months before her death she said prophetically:

Making God loved

I feel . . . that my mission is about to begin, my mission of making God loved as I love him, of giving my little way to souls . . . If God answers my desires, my heaven will be spent on earth until the end of the world . . . I want to spend my heaven in doing good on earth.

Oeuvres Complètes, Paris, 2001, p. 1050; also in Felicity Leng, *Smiles of God: The Flowers of St Thérèse of Lisieux*, London, 2003, p.142

Biographies and Bibliographies

ANGELA of Foligno (Blessed) (1248–1309)

Italian mystic

She was born into a rich family, married young and lived luxuriously. In 1285, after her husband's death, she changed her life to one of austerity and devotion, and eventually became a third-order Franciscan. She experienced intense visions, especially of Christ's sufferings. Brother Arnold, her Franciscan confessor, recorded her religious insights and teachings as she dictated them. In her *Book of Divine Consolation*, a masterpiece of early Franciscan piety, Angela describes God's summons to the soul and its ultimately successful quest for him, and stresses the importance of Christ's saving work and eucharistic presence in that progress towards God.

Liber visionum et instructionum (Alcalá, 1502); *The Book of Divine Consolation of the Blessed Angela of Foligno,* tr. Mary G. Steegman (London, 1908–9); *Le Livre des Visions de Sainte Angèle de Foligno,* ed. and tr. M. J. Ferré and L. Baudry (Paris, 1927); *Angela of Foligno, Complete Works,* tr. Paul Lachance (New York, 1993) ; L. Leclève, *Sainte Angèle de Foligno* (Paris, 1936).

ASKEW (or AYSCOUGH), Anne (1521–46)

English Protestant martyr

In the 1540s the wayward Henry VIII intensified his persecution of Protestants who professed opinions irreconcilable with whatever Catholic teachings he had decided to retain after his break with Rome. Anne Askew was married to a religious conservative, Thomas Kyme, from whom she was later separated. She was not afraid to defend her strong Reformed beliefs. She was denounced to the authorities (perhaps by her husband) and questioned rigorously in 1545 by Bishops Bonner and Gardiner, who tried to make her recant. In 1546 she was tortured by privy councillors trying to obtain information about influential Protestants at Court, and burnt at Smithfield. Her descriptions of her two interrogations were smuggled to Germany, published there by the reformer John Bale, and later included in John Foxe's *Acts and Monuments* (1563) (*Foxe's Book of Martyrs*).

The First Examination of the worthy Servant of God, Mistress Anne Askew lately martyred in Smithfield, ed. J. Bale (Marburg, 1546); *The Latter Examination of Anne Askew*, ed. J. Bale (Marburg, 1547); *The Account of the Sufferings of Anne Askew . . . written by herself* (London, 1849); *The Examinations of Anne Askew*, ed. E. V. Beilin (London, 1996); T. Betteridge, 'Anne Askew, John Bale, and Protestant History', *Journal of Medieval and Early Modern Studies*, 27 (1997), 265–84.

BASHKIRTSEFF, Marie (1860–84)

Russian diarist and painter

A Russian who wrote in French, she was born at Poltava in the Ukraine and left Russia when ten to visit Austria, Germany, Switzerland and France. She lived with some members of her extended family and a few servants in Nice and later Paris, from the age of twelve, when she began her journal. She set herself a daily nine-hour study programme. She visited Rome with her father. In spite of many arrangements and offers, she refused to marry 'for the sake of marriage'. She dreamed of becoming a singer but lost her singing voice in 1876. She entered the Académie Julian in Paris in 1877 and dedicated herself to art: 'you no longer have a family name, and cease to be your mother's child: you become yourself, an individual, with nothing but art as your goal'. In that year she learned that she was under sentence of death and worked more intensely than ever before to define and express 'that spark, that supreme mystery, that something divine which we have in us'. Some of her paintings are in leading French museums. She also wrote, under a pseudonym, for a feminist paper. She became deaf in 1880. She made the last entries in her remarkable diary eleven days before her death from tuberculosis. It was published posthumously in 1887.

Marie Bashkirtseff, *Journal* (Paris, 1887); *Lettres* (Paris, 1891); *Cahiers intimes inédits (1873–1882)* 4 vols (Paris, 1925); *Journal de Marie Bashkirtseff*, 2 vols (Paris, 1955); Colette Cosnier, *Marie Bashkirtseff. Un portrait sans retouches* (Paris, 1985).

BEAUMONT, Agnes (1652–1720)

English Nonconformist and spiritual writer

Agnes Beaumont lived with her father John in Edworth, Bedfordshire. He died in February 1674, in the year when she composed her spiritual narrative, an unusually straightforward account of her relationship with God before and at the time of her persecution. Agnes wanted to attend a meeting at Gamlinghay but had no means of doing so. John Bunyan, then pastor of the Bedford congregation, offered to take her. Malicious rumours about Bunyan were already circulating. John Beaumont forbade her to attend the meeting. When she disobeyed him, for some days he forced her to spend the night in the barn or with her brother. Eventually she was allowed back into the house. Shortly afterwards her father died of a heart attack. The villainous Feery, one of Agnes's former admirers, accused her of murdering her father. She was rumoured to be 'a witch, a Jesuit, a highwayman, and the like'. Agnes was put on trial but convinced the jury of her innocence. She was married twice, died in Highgate in 1720 aged 68, and was interred in the Baptist cemetery at Hitchin.

Real Religion: exemplified in the singular experience and great sufferings of Agnes Beaumont, of Edworth, in the County of Bedford (n.p., 1801); *The Narrative of the Persecution of Agnes Beaumont: A Diary*, ed. G. B. Harrison (London, n.d.).

BERNADETTE of Lourdes (St) (1844–79)

French visionary

Bernadette Soubirous was a poor, minimally educated miller's daughter, born at Lourdes in the Hautes-Pyrénées region of

France. On several occasions in 1858, while she was tending sheep on the mountainside, our Lady appeared and talked to her. Among other 'instructions', Mary told Bernadette to strike a certain spot where a seemingly miraculous spring of water gushed out. The water apparently had great healing power and miracles were acclaimed. At first there was great excitement but also much scepticism at Bernadette's revelations. An enquiry was held, which resulted in Rome declaring that the apparitions were genuine. Bernadette became a Sister of Notre Dame in 1866 and lived a life of pious obscurity. Her reports and the apparitions inspired a movement of intense devotion, prayer and pilgrimage that spread throughout France, Europe and the world. Although this particular kind of piety faded gradually from World War I onwards, Bernadette was beatified and canonized, and Lourdes remains one of the world's great healing shrines and centres of pilgrimage.

Lourdes, Documents authentiques, ed. R. Laurentin, B. Billet and P. Galland (Paris, 1958 ff.); *Les Ecrits de Sainte Bernadette et sa voie spirituelle*, ed. A. Ravier SJ (Paris, 1961); *Logia de Bernadette*, ed. R. Laurentin and M.-T. Bourgeade, 3 vols (Paris, 1971); F. P. Keyes, *Bernadette of Lourdes* (London, 1953); Francis Trochu, *Sainte Bernadette Soubirous* (London, 1957); L.-J.-M. Cros and P. M. Olphe-Galliard SJ, *Lourdes 1858* (Paris, 1957); R. Laurentin, Bernadette of Lourdes (London, 1979); A. Ravier, *Bernadette Soubirous* (Paris, 1979); Ruth Harris, *Lourdes* (London, 1999).

BRIDGET of Sweden (St) (1303–73)

Foundress, visionary and reformer

Born into a wealthy and very devout family near Stockholm, she had her first vision aged seven, and was granted revelations throughout her life. When she was thirteen she was married to a nobleman and went on to have eight children. In 1341 the couple went on pilgrimage to Compostella. After her husband's death almost a year later, her revelations led her to call for the papacy to leave Avignon and return to Rome, and for a reform of spiritual life in the Church. She was also instructed to found the Order of the Most Holy Saviour (the Brigittine Order), a dual community of nuns and priests. She was helped in this by her daughter, St Catherine of Sweden. She moved to Rome in 1349. She was a major influence on rulers of her times. Her revelations had a high reputation in the Middle Ages. She was canonized by Pope Boniface IX in 1391.

Revelationes Extravagantes, ed. C. Durante, 2 vols (Rome, 1628); *Revelationes Extrauagantes*, ed. L. Hollman (Uppsala, 1956); Birgitta of Sweden, *The Life and Selected Revelations of Birgitta of Sweden*, ed. M. T. Harris, tr. A. R. Kezel (New York and Mahwah, NJ, 1990); H. Redpath, *God's Ambassadress – St Bridget of Sweden* (Milwaukee, 1947).

BRONTË, Emily Jane (1818–48)

English mystico-romantic novelist and poet

The short-lived Emily Brontë was one of three sisters whose father Patrick, of Irish ancestry, was a Yorkshire curate before being appointed rector of Haworth in 1820. The three sisters and their brother lived in a hothouse atmosphere of intense reading and mutual fostering of the imagination in the lonely rectory. Emily was educated at home, and for one year in Lancashire, and taught for a short time in Halifax. In 1842 she accompanied her sister Charlotte (author of *Jane Eyre*) to Brussels to learn French and how to run a school. Charlotte was impressed by Emily's verse when she came across her work unexpectedly. Poems by Emily, Charlotte and Ann were published as written by 'Currer, Ellis and Acton Bell'. Emily's extraordinarily lyrical and passionate novel *Wuthering Heights* was published in 1847. She died of consumption in December 1848.

Poems by Currer, Ellis, and Acton Bell (London, 1846); *The Complete Poems of Emily Brontë*, ed. C. W. Hatfield (New York, 1941); Emily Jane Brontë, *Gondal Poems*, ed. H. Brown and J. Mott (Oxford, 1938); A. Robinson and F. Mary, *Emily Brontë* (1883, 1978); V. Moore, *The Life and Eager Death of Emily Brontë* (London, 1936); F. Goodridge, *Emily Brontë: Wuthering Heights* (London, 1967); Katherine Frank, *A Chainless Soul* (London, 1990).

CATHERINE of Genoa (St) (1447–1510)

She was born into the Fieschi family of leading Genoese aristo-crats. Renowned for her beauty and intelligence, at sixteen she was married to the unfaithful and spendthrift Giuliano Adorni. In 1473, after a profound religious conversion, she worked at the Pammatone Hospital for the poor, with special devotion dur-ing the fever epidemic of 1493. Her now impoverished husband joined her, eventually became a Franciscan tertiary and died in 1497. Catherine directed the hospital from 1490 to 1496. She had a series of religious experiences and led a life of penance. In 1499 she came under the influence of a spiritual director, Cataneo Marabotto. *Purgation and Purgatory* and *The Spiritual Dialogue* are posthumous compilations from Marabotto's and other friends' records of her conversations and teachings.

Vita e dottrina di S. da Caterina da Genova ([1551], Genoa, n.d.); *Catherine of Genoa, Purgation and Purgatory, The Spiritual Dialogue*, tr. Serge Hughes (New York, 1979–80); F. von Hügel, *The Mystical Element of Religion as Studied in Saint Catherine of Genoa and Her Friends*, 2 vols (London, 1908); Umile da Genoa, OM Cap, *S. Caterina Fieschi Adorni*, 2 vols (Milan, 1961–2).

CATHERINE of Siena (St) (1347–80)
Italian Doctor of the Church

Caterina Benincasa was born in Siena as the twenty-third of a wealthy dyer's twenty-five children. She made a vow of perpetual virginity for Jesus' sake when she was twelve. When sixteen, she became a Dominican lay sister. After three years of seclusion at home, she decided to devote herself, together with a 'family' of men and women, clerics and lay folk, to looking after the sick and poor and converting sinners. She was soon asked to medi-ate in disputes between local groups, and even in Florence and the Holy See. Members of her 'family' travelled with her on her diplomatic missions. She dictated an immense number of letters, of which 383 survive, on behaviour and public affairs, such as a crusade against the Turks and the Great Schism. Major topics of her writings are the unity of the Church and the crucified Christ, especially the concept of his Blood, which she presented as the main sign of God's love and the reason for our own reciprocation of it. She helped to persuade Pope Gregory XI to move the papacy from Avignon to Rome in 1377. She died on 29 April 1380, aged 33. Many commentators say this was a result of the agony she suffered over the Great Schism.

St Catherine of Siena, *Dialogo*, ed. G. Cavallini (Rome, 1968); *La Verità dell' Amore* (sel. letters), ed. G. Cavallini (Rome, 1978); *I, Catherine*, tr. and ed. K. Foster OP and M. J. Ronayne OP (London, 1980); *The Letters of St Catherine of Siena*, tr. and ed. S. Noffke OP (New York, 1988).

CHANTAL, Jeanne-Françoise Frémyot de (St) (St Jane Frances de Chantal) (1572–1641)

French foundress and spiritual writer

Born into an aristocratic family in Dijon, France, in 1592 she married the Baron de Chantal and went on to have four children. She came into contact with the main trends of mysticism that developed in French Catholicism after the Tridentine reforms. After the Baron's death in 1601, with the help of St Francis de Sales (her spiritual director from 1604) she established the Order of the Visitation of the Virgin Mary at Annecy in 1610. In spite of much opposition, she founded eighty-seven convents in her own lifetime. The order welcomed widows and women whom other orders rejected because of ill-health. St Jeanne was a very sensitive person who led a mystical prayer-life which she was reluctant to describe in great detail. She was an influential spiritual director, encouraged mental prayer, and discouraged excessive demonstrations of mystical engagement. She was a constant practitioner of her charitable ideals and ensured that the needs of her order were met.

Sainte J. F. Frémyot de Chantal: Sa vie et ses oeuvres, ed. F.-M. de Chaugy, 8 vols (Paris, 1874–9); *The Spirit of St Jane de Chantal*, tr. Sisters of the Visitation (London, 1933); E. Stopp, *Saint Jane Frances de Chantal* (London, 1962); R. P. Mezard, *Doctrine spirituelle de sainte Jeanne-Françoise de Chantal* (Paris, 1980); A. Ravier, *Jeanne-Françoise Frémyot, baronne de Chantal* (Paris, 1983).

CHRISTINE, Lucie (Mathilde Bertrand) (1844–1908)

A French spiritual diarist writing as 'Lucie Christine'. She was born Mathilde Bertrand; married Thomas Boutlé, a notary public, in 1865; had five children; and in 1882 became a nun, with unknown status, of the *Adoration réparatrice* convent in Paris, as Marie-Aimée de Jésus. She was widowed in 1886. She was an introspective mystic to whom God spoke in a very private space.

Lucie Christine, *Journal spirituel* (1870–1910), ed. P. A. Poulain SJ (Paris, 1916).

DAVIES, Eleanor, Lady (1590–1652)

Anglo-Welsh prophet and visionary

Lady Davies, who described herself somewhat haughtily as 'handmaiden of the most high God of heaven . . . fifth daughter of George Lord Castlehaven', was an earl's daughter and wife of the attorney-general for Ireland. In 1625 she heeded the voice of the Prophet Daniel summoning her to what became twenty-seven years of prophecy and religious-political commentary. She sent advice on international politics to Archbishop Laud which he sent back to her husband, who promptly consigned it to the flames; she prophesied her husband's death within three years, and he died in 1626. She wrote and published anti-Laudian, that is, Puritan, tracts that were publicly burnt by the Archbishop in 1633. Among the charges brought against her were that she dared to interpret Scripture and that she falsely claimed to have received prophetic visions. In 1635 she was accused of desecrating the altar of Lichfield Cathedral and was committed to Bedlam without a trial. Later she was imprisoned in the Tower of London but was freed and spent the rest of her life in prophecy, often of the impending death of well-known persons, and in tract writing.

C. J. Hindle, *A Bibliography of the Printed Pamphlets and Broadsides of Lady Eleanor Douglas, the Seventeenth-Century Prophetess* (Edinburgh, 1936); Esther S. Cope, *Handmaid of the Holy Spirit: Dame Eleanor Davies, Never Soe Mad a Ladie* (New York, 1992); Phyllis Mack, *Visionary Women* (Berkeley, Los Angeles and London, 1992).

DAY, Dorothy (1897–1979)

American journalist, social critic and practical Christian

Dorothy Day studied at the University of Illinois from 1914 to 1916. She joined the Socialist Party, wrote for socialist newspapers in New York, and became a member of the Industrial Workers of the World (IWW). Her compassionate heart and interest in religion eventually led her into the Roman Catholic Church (1927). She was immensely impressed by the thinking of the social critic Peter Maurin, whom she met in 1932, and by his 'green revolution', a proposed solution for the chaos and poverty of the 'dustbowl' years in the USA. He advocated a system of communal farms and houses of hospitality for the urban poor, and a programme of debate, discussion, exchange of information and experience, and joint action by blue-collar and white-collar workers and other committed Catholics in cities and on the land. Day and Maurin opened St Joseph's House of Hospitality for down-and-outs and the impoverished in New York, which was the first of several such houses across the USA. In 1933 they started the *Catholic Worker*, an inexpensive monthly newspaper, to spread their ideas and as a vehicle for a radical socio-anarchist Catholicism which seemed to draw equally on the papal 'social encyclicals' and romantic Marxism. Within three years the paper's circulation was 150,000. Day became a much-loved mother-figure of radical Catholicism by the time of Vatican II. She opposed the Vietnam War, supported Cesar Chavez and his United Farm Workers, and was arrested in 1973 during a demonstration on their behalf.

Dorothy Day, *The Long Loneliness: An Autobiography* (New York, 1952); Deborah Kent, *Dorothy Day: Friend of the Forgotten* (New York, 1996).

DHUODA (c. 803–43)

French writer on morality and devotion

Dhuoda lived and wrote during the Carolingian period in France. She spent most of her life in exile in the Provencal town of Uzès. She was deserted by her husband, Bernard, Duke of Septimania, who took their son, William, to live with him. When William was sixteen, she wrote a 'manual' or spiritual self-help book for his daily use. Dhuoda wanted it to be 'a mirror in which he could contemplate the salvation of his soul'. In this guide she reveals her faith, motherly tenderness, culture and experience. She advises William how to behave with regard not only to God, the Church, his father, family, King and court but also to the poor and ordinary people. She accompanies these sound instructions with a mixture of family memories, poems and prayers, and describes her worries about her sons in such troubled times as well as her own sufferings.

Dhuoda, *Manuel pour mon Fils*, ed. Pierre Riché (Paris, 1997); *Handbook for William: A Carolingian Woman's Counsel for Her Son*, tr. Carol Neel (Washington, DC, 1991).

DICKINSON, Emily (1830–86)

American poet and mystic

Emily Elizabeth Dickinson was one of three children. She was educated at Amherst Academy and Mount Holyoke Female Seminary. She was sceptical about official religion, but experienced intense emotions that can only be described as religious and/or mystical. Many of her poems ostensibly (and many implicitly) concern God, the love of Christ and Emily's mystical union with him. Her first poems were inspired by Emerson, the American 'transcendentalists', and Emily Brontë. Charles Wadsworth, a Calvinist preacher, became her correspondent and 'dearest earthly friend', and influenced her thinking. She gradually developed a highly concentrated metaphysical wit and a 'haiku'-like style unique in English-language literature, which enabled her to combine multiple views of profound universal mysteries with hints of personal joys and dilemmas. After developing severe eye problems in 1864–5 she became somewhat reclusive, and dressed always in white. Only seven of her poems appeared while she was alive. Her sister made sure that most of her work was published posthumously.

Poems by Emily Dickinson, 1st, 2nd and 3rd series, ed. M. L. Todd and T. W. Higginson (Boston, 1890, 1891, 1896); *The Complete Poems of Emily Dickinson*, ed. Thomas H. Johnson (London, 1970); Martha Bianchi

Dickinson, *The Life and Letters of Emily Dickinson* (Boston, 1924); Emily Dickinson, *Bolts of Melody*, ed. M. L. Todd and M. T. Bingham (New York, 1945); Jay Leyda, *The Years and Hours of Emily Dickinson*, 2 vols (New York, 1960).

EDDY, Mary Baker (1821–1910)

American theologian and speculative religious writer, founder of Christian Science

She was born to Congregationalist parents in New Hampshire, USA. Mary's ill-health, primarily a spinal problem, meant she had little formal education, but she was affected by the more popular currents of New England transcendentalism. Her first husband died before the birth of their son, who was raised by others. She became interested in homoeopathy and in 1853 married Daniel Paterson, a dentist of that persuasion. She was impressed and helped by the healing methods of Phineas P. Quimby, who used no medicines but seemed to have rediscovered Jesus' own approach. Her sickness returned after his death. After a fall on the ice in 1866 an extraordinary curative experience showed her how to remain in good health and how to heal others. She was separated from her husband and for several years developed and wrote about what she called Christian Science, which she taught as a system to change thinking and thus lead to health. In 1875 she published *Science and Health*, revised before her death as *Science and Health with Key to the Scriptures*. In 1877 she married Asa G. Eddy, one of her disciples. In 1879 Christian Science became the belief system of an influential church. Mrs Eddy founded several papers, including the *Christian Science Monitor*.

Mary Baker Eddy, *Science and Health with Key to the Scriptures* (Boston, 1875); *Miscellaneous Writings* (Boston, 1896); *Retrospection and Introspection* (Boston, 1892); Robert Peel, *Mary Baker Eddy: The Years of Authority* (New York, 1977).

EVANS, Margiad (1909–58)

Anglo-Welsh quietist, mystic, diarist and novelist

Margiad Evans was born in Uxbridge near London, but when she was quite young her family moved to near Ross-on-Wye in Herefordshire. She was deeply affected by the border landscape, and its features became Romantic metaphors for her states of body and mind. In the 1950s she suffered from epilepsy and her illness also became a source of metaphor for her mystical apprehensions of a reality within yet beyond the circumambient world. She described her sickness in *A Ray of Darkness*. Although she was impressed by diverse writers such as Herbert, Vaughan, Blake, Emily Brontë and Thoreau, her ability to transcribe the private messages of the natural world for others is unique.

Margiad Evans, *Autobiography* (London, 1943); *Country Dance* (London, 1932); *The Wooden Doctor* (Oxford, 1933); *A Ray of Darkness* (London, 1952).

FELL, Margaret (1614–1702)

English devotional writer and religious activist

Margaret Fell, known as the 'Nurturing Mother' of Quakerism, was born in Dalton, Lancashire. She married Thomas Fell, a barrister, and had eight children. Her marital home, Swarthmoor Hall, was the early headquarters of the Friends. She said that the first twenty years of her marriage were spent seeking the best ways to serve God. Travelling ministers, including George Fox, stayed at her home. In 1658 her husband died and in 1659 Fox was arrested at Margaret's house and imprisoned. She obtained his release. After renewed persecution of the Quakers, Margaret secured a proclamation of freedom to Quakers from the King and Council, but in 1664 her house was ransacked, Fox again imprisoned, and Margaret herself arrested for refusing to take an oath to the King. She was tried, and sentenced to life imprisonment and forfeiture of her property. During four and a half years in gaol she wrote many pamphlets before her release in 1668. She was imprisoned again but eventually, in 1686, James II issued the Act of Toleration and all Quakers were freed from prison.

Margaret Fell, *A Brief Collection of Remarkable Passages and Occurrences Relating to the Birth, Education, Life, Conversion, Travels, Services and Deep Sufferings of That Ancient, Eminent and Faithful Servant of the Lord, Margaret Fell, but by Her Second Marriage, Margaret Fox* (London, 1710); *Women's Speaking Justified, Proved and Allowed of by the Scriptures, All Such as Speak by the Spirit and Power of the Lord Jesus. And How Women Were the First That Preached the Tidings of the Resurrection of Jesus, and Were Sent by Christ's Own Command Before He Ascended to the Father* (pamphlet, London, n.d.); Helen G. Crosfield, *Margaret Fox of Swarthmoor Hall* (London, 1913); Bonnelyn Young Kunze, *Margaret Fell and the Rise of Quakerism* (New York, 1994).

FRY, Elizabeth (1780–1845)

English evangelist and social reformer

Elizabeth Gurney was the daughter of a Quaker banker, and was born in Norwich. She married Joseph Fry, a London merchant, and had several children. She founded a girls' school and, when twenty-nine, became a Quaker 'minister' and a welcome preacher. She was a dedicated evangelist but most interested in practical charity and social reform. Her position in society allowed her to contact influential people who could help her in the long and often successful campaign to reform prisons which she started in 1813. She required the separation of the sexes, women warders for women prisoners, and education and religious instruction in gaols. She also fought to improve the treatment of urban vagrants and beggars. In 1839 she started a criminal rehabilitation society. She also founded an order of nursing sisters. Fry was responsible for an influential report on social conditions in Ireland and helped to set up libraries at coastguard stations, in naval hospitals and elsewhere.

Memoir of the Life of Elizabeth Fry with Extracts from her Journal and Letters, ed. two of her daughters, 2 vols (London, 1848); J. Kent, *Elizabeth Fry* (London, 1962).

GERTRUDE of Helfta (St) (Gertude the Great) (1256–1301/2)

German mystic and devotional writer

From the age of five, Gertrude lived with the nuns to whom she was 'offered' at the convent of Helfta in Thuringia, where, in spite of her initially 'half-hearted' enthusiasm, she learned Latin, philosophy and theology and came under the influence of the abbess's sister, St Mechthild. When about twenty-five, she experienced her first visions of Jesus as a boy of sixteen, in which he reproached her for neglecting prayer in favour of study. For the most part, her mystical experiences occurred during divine worship, and the liturgical offices, as well as the Song of Songs and St John, influenced their language. She was an early writer on devotion to the Sacred Heart of Jesus, which was a central topic of some of her visions. Her revelations were recorded in her *Legate of Divine Love* (composed partly from her notes). She wrote a popular book of prayers. She was canonized by 'acclamation' but her feast was officially authorized.

Gertrude of Helfta, *The Herald of Divine Love*, tr. M. Winkworth (New York and Mahwah, NJ, 1993); G. Ledos, *Sainte Gertrude* (Paris, 1904).

GÖRRES, Ida Friederike (1901–71)

Diarist and writer

Ida Görres was born into a German-speaking family in Bohemia, Austria (now the Czech Republic). She was one of the seven children of Count Heinrich Coudenhove, diplomatist, linguist and student of comparative religion, and his Japanese wife, Misu Aoyama. After her father's early death, her invalid mother, with the help of nurses and governesses, raised her in accordance with then-fashionable 'Anglophile' ideas. She was educated in an IBVM convent, and, for a short time, 'tried her vocation as a nun but realized that her true calling was in lay activities'. She studied at Vienna and Freiburg universities. She became involved in social work and was a leading figure of the Catholic League of the German Youth Movement before Hitler took power in 1933. In 1935 she married Carl Josef Görres. Catholic writing was censored under the Nazi regime, but she was able to lecture to adult and youth groups, and to the incipient ecumenical movement. After the war, as outspoken lay Catholicism was freed from previous restrictions, she lectured, broadcast and wrote for journals.

In 1950 she suffered a breakdown, and wrote books in virtual retirement. All her works are concerned with human nature and its function in the universe.

Ida Friederike Görres, *The Hidden Face: A Study of St Thérèse of Lisieux* (London, 1959); *Broken Lights*, tr. Barbara Waldstein-Wartenberg (London, 1964).

GRIFFITHS, Ann (1776–1805)
Welsh hymn writer and mystic

We have about thirty Welsh hymns handed down by oral tradition and a handful of letters in Welsh (the language she spoke and wrote in) by Ann Griffiths, the daughter of a tenant farmer and churchwarden (of the local Anglican church) in the Berwyns, Wales. After her mother's death when Ann was eighteen, she ran the household, cooking and spinning for her father, and lived the everyday life of a small farm. She was converted to Methodism during the great evangelistic revival that swept through North Wales in the late eighteenth century before the decisive split from the Church of England (in 1811). Ann married a Methodist farmer, but less than a year later when she was twenty-nine, died two weeks after her daughter's birth and death. Ann's commitment to her new enthusiastic form of devotion, her typically Methodist conviction of salvation, her unusually intense longing for God, and her constant awareness of his transcendence and of her own transience brought her a reputation for holiness and, indeed, saintliness.

Gwaith Ann Griffiths, ed. Owen M. Edwards (Conwy, 1905); *Ann Griffiths, A Short Memoir of Ann Griffiths with a Translation of her Letters and Hymns*, tr. E. Richards (Cardiff, 1916); *The Hymns of Ann Griffiths*, ed. John Ryan, tr. Robert O. F. Wynne and John Ryan (Bontnewydd, 1980); A. M. Allchin, *Ann Griffiths* (Cardiff, 1976); James Coutts, ed., *Homage to Ann Griffiths* (Penarth, 1976).

GUYON, Jeanne-Marie Bouvier de La Motte-Guyon
(1648–1717)

French writer on matters spiritual and religious

Jeanne Guyon was disliked by her mother and mother-in-law and experienced much of her life as a 'series of misfortunes'. Her spiritual director helped her to abandon an uninspired and conventional piety and to explore a gift for mystical inwardness. This issued in a totally new life for this obscure wife, then widow, of a provincial gentleman. She began to lead a peripatetic life between Savoy, where she met a new source of religious inspiration, Fr La Combe, a Barnabite friar, and Paris, where she encountered the theologian Fénélon and became a leading figure in the Quietist movement. In 1681 she set off with La Combe to preach Quietist Christianity throughout France. In 1685 the Inquisition imprisoned Miguel de Molinos, the Spanish founder of the tendency, and in 1687 Guyon and La Combe were arrested for suspected heresy. Molinos was sentenced to life imprisonment and his teachings were condemned. The influential writer Mme de Maintenon managed to arrange for Guyon's release. Though favoured by the Court, Guyon had to ask for clearance by a theological commission. She was condemned by the Conference of Issy, gaoled in various convents and the Bastille (1695–1702), and freed only when she announced her submission. Her writings fill thirty-nine volumes.

La Vie de Mme J.-M. Bouvier de La Motte Guyon écrite par lui-même (Cologne, 1720); Mme Guyon, *Vie* (Paris, 1983); *Autobiography*, tr. T. T. Allen, 2 vols (London, 1897); Françoise Mallet-Joris, *Jeanne Guyon* (Paris, 1978).

HADEWIJCH (*fl.* 1230–50)

Flemish poet, mystic and visionary

Hadewijch lived in the Duchy of Brabant in the second quarter of the thirteenth century and wrote in the local dialect. Her *Visions* and letters seem to show that she was a Beguine. She was well educated and knew the Latin Bible, theology, and even some French romances. She writes for those (presumably Beguines) who wish to know how to unite their souls with a loving God who is greater than all possibilities of possession and union. Her letters were cited by Ruysbroeck in the fourteenth century and were translated into High German. Some manuscripts were definitely ascribed to her in the early nineteenth century. The authorship of some poems formerly (and some still) attributed to her is uncertain.

Het Visionenboek van Hadewijch, ed. P. H. Vekeman (Nijmegen and Bruges, 1979); Hadewich, *Lettres spirituelles* (Geneva, 1971); *Hadewijch: The Complete Works*, tr. and ed. Mother Columba Hart OSB (New York and London, 1980); J. B. Porion, *Hadewijch d'Anvers* (Paris, 1954).

HILDEGARD of Bingen (1098–1179)

German abbess, healer, counsellor, poet, theologian and mystic prophet

When she was eight, Hildegard was dedicated to the religious life and entered a small Benedictine monastery close to her home. She proved to be a ready learner and assimilated a vast amount of Scripture, theology, natural science, cosmology, and medical and natural lore which gradually issued forth in practical, theoretical and mystico-literary works. She was an influential nun and her sisters elected her abbess in 1136. Eventually she moved her community to Rupertsberg near Bingen, where she built a much larger convent. She became a religious adviser to powerful people and a counsellor to all sorts and conditions of men and women. Her writing covers an immense variety of subjects including hagiography, sermons, medicine, marital and sexual recommendations, and natural history. She was a fine poet and composed liturgical music. She is mainly celebrated for her visionary works.

The Life and Visions of St. Hildegarde, ed. and tr. Francisca Maria Steele (London, 1914); Heinrich Schipperges, *The World of Hildegard of Bingen: Her Life, Times and Visions*, tr. J. Cumming (London, 1997); Renate Craine, *Hildegard, Prophet of the Cosmic Christ* (New York, 1997).

HOUSELANDER, Caryll (1901–1954)

English spiritual writer and counsellor

Frances Caryll Houselander nearly died at birth. She was formally baptized only when six. She experienced a mysterious illness when seven, but recovered immediately after receiving the last anointing. This resulted in a lifelong devotion to Jesus and Catholicism. She was deeply upset by her parents' separation when she was nine. Throughout her childhood she suffered from continual bad health, and although she was sent to various convent schools her education suffered from the illnesses that kept her out of the classroom. As an adolescent, she had the first of three visions which, she felt, summoned her to 'see Christ in all people'. She attended art school, and developed her gift for illustration. She became a firm Catholic when twenty-four. She developed a gift for spiritual healing and a well-known psychiatrist sent her patients whom she 'loved back to life'. She wrote letters to the many correspondents who came to depend on her for consolation. Her books and articles have helped many people in psychic need.

Caryll Houselander, *This War is the Passion* (New York, 1941; London, 1943); *The Reed of God* (London, 1944); *The Flowering Tree* (London, 1945); *Guilt* (New York, 1951; London, 1952); *A Rocking-Horse Catholic* (London and New York, 1955); *The Letters of Caryll Houselander: Her Spiritual Legacy*, ed. Maisie Ward (London and New York, 1965).

HROSWITHA (or Hrosvit) of Gandersheim (c. 935–c. 1000)

German poet, dramatist, hagiographer and moralist

Hroswitha was born to a noble Christian family early in the tenth century. She was probably very young when she entered the highly selective and prestigious abbey at Gandersheim, in Saxony, which was reserved for aristocrats' daughters. Eventually she became a canoness, having taken vows of celibacy and obedience, but not poverty. Gandersheim was a much-respected abbey, with a strong reputation for education and the devotional life, and Hroswitha's writings show a wide-ranging knowledge of Latin classics and Scripture and an ability to manipulate literary genres and formal structures. Gandersheim maintained an army, had a court for legal disputes and produced its own coinage. Hroswitha cherished her writing ability, which she devoted to morally improving yet stylistically and structurally interesting verse, dramas and tales, in which firmly upheld chastity was a recurrent topic.

Hroswitha of Gandersheim, *Plays*, ed. and tr. Katharina M. Wilson (Saskatoon, 1986; rev. edn New York and London, 1989); A. L. Haight, ed., *Hroswitha of Gandersheim* (New York, 1965); Peter Dronke, *Women Writers of the Middle Ages* (Cambridge, 1984); K. M. Wilson, *Hroswitha of Gandersheim* (Leiden, 1988).

HUTCHINSON, Lucy (1620–*c*. 1675)

English devotional writer, scholar and translator

Lucy Apsley, a devout, scholarly Puritan, was the daughter of Sir Allen Apsley, Lieutenant-Governor of the Tower of London, and was born there on 29 January 1620. She married the republican hero John Hutchinson in 1638. She wrote her memoirs of her husband between 1664 and 1671 to vindicate their joint attempt, with others, to overthrow the King and set up an England that would mirror divine government as they interpreted it. From the age of four she could speak French and 'read English perfectly'. An excellent Latinist, she was so fond of books when young that her mother hid them for her health's sake. She was influenced by John Owen and other thinkers of the 1640s–50s, and was well versed in Neo-Platonism. She translated Owen's *Theologoumena pantodapa* and Latin classics. She wrote *On the Principles of the Christian Religion* for her daughter's edification, other theological pieces, the discursive verse work *Order and Disorder*, and several elegies.

Lucy Hutchinson, *Memoirs of the Life of Colonel Hutchinson* (London, 1806); *Memoirs of Colonel Hutchinson* with a preface by François Guizot (London, 1908); *Memoirs of the Life of Colonel Hutchinson with a fragment of autobiography*, ed. N. H. Keeble (London, 1995); *Order and disorder; or the world made and undone, being meditations on the creation and fall; as it is recorded in the beginning of Genesis* (London, 1679); *Order and Disorder*, ed. D. Norbrook (London, 2001).

JULIAN of Norwich (1342–*c.* 1416)

English spiritual writer

She was an anchoress (living in considerable physical restriction) near the church of St Julian the Hospitaller in Norwich, and author of the first book in English certainly written by a woman. This work, *Sixteen Revelations of Divine Love*, has come down to us as two texts, one short, one long, in later manuscript versions. It was based on her mystical visions in 1373 and has one essential theme: the nature and irresistible power of the love of God. Julian is convinced that God means love; that this love keeps everything in being; and that, ultimately, everything in the universe will be for the best. Her description of the Trinity as Father, Mother and Lord leads into her presentation of divine love as motherly, and of Christ's suffering on the cross as the pains of a woman in childbirth. This aspect of her work has proved especially attractive to modern, and above all feminist, theologians.

Julian of Norwich, *Revelations of Divine Love*, tr. Grace Warrack (London, 1901); *Revelations of Divine Love*, tr. R. Hudleston (London, 1927); *Revelations of Divine Love*, tr. C. Wolters (Harmondsworth, 1966); *Showings*, ed. and tr. E. Colledge OSA and J. Walsh SJ (London, 1978); Paul Molinari, *Julian of Norwich* (London, 1958); Matthew Fox, *Original Blessing* (Santa Fe, 1983); Grace M. Jantzen, *Julian of Norwich: Mystic and Theologian* (London, 1987); Frodo Okulam, *The Julian Mystique* (Mystic, 1998).

KEMPE, Margery (1373–*c.* 1438)

English autobiographer, religious and travel writer

Margery Kempe was a cheerful, earthy mystic and a person of considerable compassion and religious insight. She was the daughter of John Burnham, mayor of Lynn on several occasions. She was born in King's Lynn, Norfolk, married John Kempe in 1393, and had fourteen children. She suffered a serious breakdown, went with her husband on pilgrimage to Canterbury, and was accused of Lollardy. In 1413 she and her husband took formal vows of chastity. She went on most adventurous pilgrimages to Italy, the Holy Land and Compostela, and visited Norway and Danzig. She recorded her religious observations and experiences in the work known as *The Book of Margery Kempe*. She received advice from her older contemporary Julian of Norwich.

The Book of Margery Kempe: A Modern Version, tr. W. Butler-Bowdon (London, 1936); *The Book of Margery Kempe*, tr. B. A. Windeatt (Harmondsworth, 1985); David Knowles, *The English Mystical Tradition* (London, 1961); C. W. Atkinson, *Mystic and Pilgrim: The Book and the World of Margery Kempe* (London, 1983).

LATASTE, Marie (1822–47)

French visionary

Marie Lataste was born to humble and devout parents in the village of Mimbaste in the Landes of Gascony. Between the ages of fourteen and twenty she had visions of Jesus and our Lady at Mass. In 1842 her parish priest persuaded her to put her visions into writing. In 1844 she went to Paris and became a lay sister in the Society of the Sacred Heart, founded by Mlle Barat, now St Madeleine Sophie. She died three years after her admission. Her writings were published in 1862–6 with episcopal approval and attestations by Jesuits that the published versions were faithful reproductions of the autographed manuscripts. Marie herself qualified the way in which she described her visions by saying: 'I have not spoken as the Saviour spoke, but as far as I have known how, and as he has permitted me.' During a period of danger and persecution of the religious orders in France, her remains were taken to England and reburied under the altar of the chapel at the Sacred Heart Convent, Digby Stuart College, Roehampton, near London.

Letters and Writings of Marie Lataste, tr. Edward Healy Thompson, 3 vols (London, 1894); *The Life of Marie Lataste, lay sister of the congregation of the Sacred Heart*, ed. and tr. E. H. Thompson (London, 1877).

MARITAIN, Raïssa (1883–1960)

French poet and spiritual writer

Raïssa Oumansov was born into an Orthodox Jewish family at Rostov-on-Don. Her father was a tailor who emigrated to France, where Raïssa acquired French nationality. In 1900 she entered the university, where she met the philosopher Jacques Maritain, a fellow-student. They married in 1904. In a joint quest for truth, they came under the influence of the writers Charles Péguy and Léon Bloy and the philosopher Henri Bergson. They were converted to Catholicism and became members of the Benedictine Third Order. Their household developed as a centre for discussions between thinkers, writers and artists, and as a workshop of practical contemplation and the application of the philosophy of St Thomas Aquinas to contemporary issues.

Oeuvres complètes de Jacques et Raïssa Maritain (Fribourg and Paris, 1982); R. Maritain, *Journal de Raïssa* (Paris, 1963); *Poèmes et Essais* (Paris, 1968); Judith D. Suther, *Raïssa Maritain, Pilgrim, Poet, Exile* (New York, 1988).

MECHTHILD of Magdeburg (*c.* 1208–82/97)

German Beguine and visionary

Mechthild was born into a wealthy aristocratic family, and was well educated although she never studied Latin or theology. She became a nun while young and was granted mystical experiences from the age of twelve, but for some thirty years remained silent about them. She had taken notes after each mystical encounter, and in about 1250 her Dominican confessor persuaded her to dictate vivid accounts of her visions. In 1270 she joined the Cistercian monastery of Helfta. Her work is said to have influenced Dante and was very influential among the Dominicans until the beginning of the sixteenth century.

Mechthild of Magdeburg, *Offenbarungen der Schwester M.v.M. oder das fliessende Licht der Gottheit*, ed. G. Morel (Regensburg, 1869; Darmstadt, 1976); *Das fliessende Licht der Gottheit*, ed. M. Schmidt (Einsiedeln &c., 1955); *La lumière de la divinité. Révélations* (Paris, 1878); *Revelations of Mechthild of Magdeburg or the flowing light of the Godhead*, tr. Lucy Menzies (London, 1953).

MEYNELL, Alice (1847–1922)

English poet and essayist

Alice Meynell was born in Barnes, London, but spent most of her youth in Italy. She became a Roman Catholic in 1872. Most of her writing was on religion and associated topics. She had a fine musical ear and many of her superbly controlled lyrics are treasured by poets for the 'dark vibrations of the sightless skies, / The lovely inexplicit colours . . .' In 1877 she married Wilfrid Meynell (1852–1948), the founder and editor of *Merry England*, a Catholic paper for which she wrote. They took up the cause of the unfortunate poet Francis Thompson, who also contributed to their magazine. She wrote fine critical essays on seventeenth-century poets and other nineteenth-century poets.

Alice Meynell, *Mary, the Mother of Jesus* (London, 1912); *Poems*, ed. F. Meynell (London, 1947); Viola Meynell, *Alice Meynell: A Memoir* (London, 1929); J. Badeni, *The Slender Tree: A Life of Alice Meynell* (Padstow, 1981).

MOTT, Lucretia (1793–1880)

Quaker minister and rights campaigner

Lucretia was an outspoken Quaker campaigner for women's rights and prominent in the anti-slavery movement in mid-nineteenth-century America. She was born into a Quaker family as Lucretia Coffin in Nantucket, Massachusetts. She became a Quaker minister in 1821. Like many Quakers, Lucretia was active in the abolitionist movement in the USA before the Civil War. She helped to found two anti-slavery groups, and was celebrated for her well-constructed and highly effective speeches against slavery. In 1840 she attended the World Anti-Slavery Convention in London. The convention was organized and controlled by men, who refused to seat her and other women delegates. Mott pledged to work consistently for women's rights. In 1848 she and Elizabeth Cady Stanton organized the first women's rights convention at Seneca Falls, New York. The meeting produced a number of resolutions calling for increased rights for women, including better opportunities for education and in employment, and the right to vote. In later years, Lucretia spoke on many occasions for the abolition of slavery and for women's rights. Her *Discourse on Women* (1850) examined educational, economic and political restrictions on women's activities in Europe and the

USA. After the abolition of slavery in 1865, Lucretia campaigned for the vote for African Americans.

Lucretia Mott: Her Complete Speeches and Sermons, ed. Dana Green (New York and Oxford, 1980); *James and Lucretia Mott: Life and Letters*, ed. Anna Davis Hallowell (Boston, 1896); J. F. Bryant, *Lucretia Mott: A Guiding Light* (New York, n.d.).

NIGHTINGALE, Florence (1820–1910)

English hospital reformer

Florence Nightingale was born in Florence, but was raised and educated in England. She trained as a nurse at Kaiserswerth and Paris. She was a devout Christian, interested in mysticism from an early age, always struggling to link 'active life and union with God', and intent on drawing practical social conclusions from religious premises. During the Crimean War, after news of shocking conditions at the front, she led a party of thirty-eight nurses to organize a nursing department at Scutari after the Battle of Alma (1854). She found the medical care and sanitation totally inadequate, and her little team was forced to look after 10,000 wounded men with minimal resources and facilities. She did everything possible to raise public awareness of the unjustified suffering of the troops and others involved in the war. She returned to England in 1856, and established an institute for training nurses. She ensured that a Royal Commission was set up to examine the whole question of army nursing. Although she suffered from chronic and debilitating brucellosis for many years, she devoted herself to her nursing college, to the training of midwives, and to campaigning for prison reform, army sanitary reform, improved nursing, and beneficial public health measures, especially in the Indian Empire.

The Collected Works of Florence Nightingale, vol. IV: *Mysticism and Eastern Religions*, ed. Gérard Vallée (Waterloo, Ont., 2005); Sir Edward Cook, *The Life of Florence Nightingale*, 2 vols (New York, 1942); Cecil Woodham-Smith, *Florence Nightingale, 1820–1910* (London, 1950); F. B. Smith, *Florence Nightingale: Reputation and Power* (London, 1982); Lytton Strachey, *Eminent Victorians* (London, 1918); Ruth Y. Jenkins, *Reclaiming Myths of Power: Women Writers and the Victorian Spiritual Crisis* (London and New York, 1996).

PARR, Katherine, Queen (1512–48)

English devotional writer

After the execution of Catherine Howard, Henry VIII married Katherine (or Catherine), the last of his six wives, on 12 July 1543. She was the daughter of a court official, Sir Thomas Parr of Kendal, and was already twice widowed. She cared for her now sick husband, and has been called more of a 'nursemaid' than a wife. She was very attentive to the education of the royal children. She was also learned and a very devout follower of the Reformed persuasion. By this point in Henry's reign, so much Catholic doctrine and practice had been eroded or abandoned that Katherine's Protestantism was not problematical, although it would have been so earlier in his life. Henry died in January 1547, and Katherine married Thomas, Lord Seymour of Sudeley, and died not long after the birth of a daughter. Her *Lamentation or Complaynt of a Sinner* was written in 1548.

Katherine Parr, *Prayers Stirring the Mind unto Heavenly Meditations Collected out of Holy Works* (London, 1545); *Lamentation of a Sinner* (London, 1548); facsimile of both works with intro. by J. Mueller: *The Early Modern Englishwoman: A facsimile library of essential works.* Part 1: Printed Writings, 1500–1640, vol. 3 (Aldershot, 1996); William P. Hangaard, 'Religious Convictions of a Renaissance Queen', *Renaissance Quarterly*, 22 (1969), pp. 346–59; Janel Mueller, 'Devotion as Difference: Intertextuality in Queen Katherine Parr's Prayers or Meditations', *Huntington Library Quarterly*, 53 (1990).

PORETE, Marguerite (12?–1310)

French theologian and religious writer, who was burnt as a heretic

Very little is known about Marguerite Porete, the author of *Le Miroeur des simples âmes*, who is presumed to have belonged to the quasi-Franciscan movement known as the Brethren of the Free Spirit. She was probably a native of Hainaut. She was burnt at the stake in Paris on 1 June 1310 for continuing to circulate copies of her book, which had already been condemned as heretical. After the unfortunate author's death, Latin, (Middle) English and Italian translations of the book, presented as versions of an anonymous minor Christian classic, were published for centuries, in Roman Catholic and other environments; the authorship and the book's 'heretical' nature were re-established only in recent years. It is a major classic (because most such works were utterly destroyed) of the school of 'Freedom of the Spirit'.

Marguerite Porete, *A Mirror for Simple Souls*, ed. C. Crawford (London, 1981); P. Dronke, *Women Writers of the Middle Ages* (London, 1981).

ROBERTS, Louisa Jewett Raymond (1819–93)
Quaker minister

Louisa Roberts was a Baptist who converted to the Society of Friends, becoming a minister in Green Street Meeting, Philadelphia. She was one of the organizers of the first day Bible schools, and an editor of the journal *Friends' Intelligencer*.

Biographical Sketch of Louisa J. Roberts with Extracts from her Journal and Selections from Her Writings (Philadelphia, 1895).

ROSSETTI, Christina (1830–94)
English poet and devotional writer

Christina Georgina Rossetti, sister of the painter and poet Dante Gabriel Rossetti, and the youngest of a family of four, was born and died in London. She published poems as 'Ellen Alleyne' in the Pre-Raphaelite journal *The Germ*. She was deeply attached to her mother, whom she helped to run an unsuccessful school in Frome, Somerset. After her father's death in 1854, Christina was somewhat impoverished. She was a devout high Anglican, and rejected Roman Catholic suitors. She entered into a close emotional relationship with the poet William Bell Scott. After the publication of *Goblin Market and Other Poems* (1862) and *The Prince's Progress and Other Poems* (1866), her intensely felt verse made her an established poet. She turned mainly to prose writing after developing a visually distressing thyroid disorder.

Poetical Works of Christina Georgina Rossetti with Memoir and Notes etc., ed. William Michael Rossetti (London, 1935); Georgina Battiscombe, *Christina Rossetti: A Divided Life* (London, 1981); Tony Castle, *The Prayers of Christina Rossetti* (London, 1989); Frances Thomas, *Christina Rossetti*

(Hanley Swan, 1992); Jan Marsh, *Christina Rossetti: A Literary Biography* (London, 1994); Mary Arseneau, *Recovering Christina Rossetti: Female Community and Incarnational Poetics* (London, 2004).

SAYERS, Dorothy Leigh (1893–1957)

English scholar and writer

Dorothy L. Sayers was the daughter of a priest of the Church of England and was born in Oxford. She read modern languages at Oxford, and was one of the first women to graduate from the University. She became an advertising copywriter, and then a famous writer of detective stories and a translator of Dante. She was also a successful Christian writer of plays, radio broadcasts and essays. Her radio play *A Man Born To Be King* was very popular and its language was acclaimed as excitingly modern. Her thinking on religion and philosophy in *The Mind of the Maker* earned her a reputation as a serious writer on religion. Her version of two-thirds of Dante's *Divine Comedy* was accepted as the standard verse translation for many years.

Dorothy L. Sayers, *The Poetry of Search and the Poetry of Statement* (London, 1963); *A Matter of Eternity: Selections from the Writings of Dorothy L. Sayers,* ed. Rosamond Kent Sprague (London, 1973); B. Reynolds, *Dorothy L. Sayers: Her Life and Soul* (London, 1993).

STANTON, Elizabeth Cady (1815–1902)

American devotional writer and early campaigner for women's rights

She was born in New York, married Henry Stanton and had seven children. She and her husband were enthusiastic anti-slavery activists, but this work showed her that even in efforts to achieve human justice women were not treated as the equals of men. Her personal interest in women's rights developed into a public campaign. She became a friend of Lucretia Mott, with whom she organized a women's rights convention at Seneca Falls in 1848. She saw the lack of women's suffrage as the fundamental obstacle to divinely required equality, and devoted much of her active life to the campaign for women's right to vote. She published *The Woman's Bible*, with commentaries by a number of well-educated women on relevant passages of Scripture.

Elizabeth Cady Stanton, Susan B. Anthony and Matilda J. Gage, eds, 'Declaration of Sentiments', in *History of Woman Suffrage* (Rochester, New York, 1881), vol. I, pp. 67–94; Elizabeth Cady Stanton, *The Woman's Bible* (New York, 1972).

STEIN, Edith (St) (1891–1942)

German theologian, philosopher, mystic, martyr and proto-feminist

Edith Stein was born into a practising Jewish family in Breslau, Germany (now Wroclaw, Poland). When fifteen, she declared herself an atheist. She later described her younger self as 'a radical feminist'. She trained as a philosopher and became the assistant of Husserl, the founder of phenomenology. One of her major interests was the nature of personality. Later she attempted to reconcile aspects of Thomism and modern critical thought. In lectures she also encouraged women to take up a career and profession, and recommended sexual education for girls. She converted to Catholicism in 1921 after reading the autobiography of St Teresa of Avila. This intensified, rather than halting, her inveterate seeking after truth. She met the French philosopher Jacques Maritain (1882–1973), and his wife Raïssa, at a conference in Juvisy, near Paris, in 1931. They became friends and a number of letters between them have been published. In 1933 she entered the Carmelite convent in Cologne, and in 1934 was clothed as Sister Teresa-Benedicta of the Cross. In 1933, when Hitler assumed full dictatorial power, she wrote a fruitless letter to Pope Pius XI to say that not only Jews but Catholics expected and hoped that the 'Church would speak out against such an abuse of Christ's name by a supposedly Christian regime'. In 1938, as a result of the anti-Jewish Nuremberg Laws, she was transferred to the Carmel of Echt in the Netherlands. In 1942, during the German occupation, she was deported to Auschwitz and murdered there. She left a considerable body of philosophical and spiritual work. She was beatified in 1987 and canonized in 1998. In 1999 she was named

co-patroness of Europe, together with St Bridget of Sweden and
St Catherine of Siena.

Collected Works of Edith Stein (Washington, DC, 1987 ff.); Edith Stein,
Essays on Women, tr. Freda Mary Oben (Washington, DC, 1987, 1996);
On the Problem of Empathy, tr. Waltraut Stein, 3rd rev. edn (Washing-
ton, DC, 1989); *Self-Portrait in Letters, 1916–1942,* tr. Josephine Koeppel
(Washington, DC, 1993); Hilda Graef, *The Scholar and the Cross: The Life
and Works of Edith Stein* (London, 1955); *Lettres d'Edith Stein, Textes de
Raïssa Maritain* (Papers of Jacques Maritain, 25 December 1992); Maria
Amata Neyer, *Edith Stein: Her Life in Photos and Documents,* tr. Waltraut
Stein (Washington, DC, 1999); S. Borden, *Edith Stein* (London and New
York, 2003).

TEN BOOM, Corrie (1892–1983)
Dutch evangelist and pacifist resistance worker

Corrie ten Boom was an unassuming Dutch Christian of Haar-
lem whose family, under the guidance of her eighty-four-year-old
father, defied the inhumane anti-Semitic and anti-Christian laws
and behaviour of the German authorities and secret police and
their Dutch official and unofficial collaborators during the occupation of the Netherlands in World War II. With the unmistakable news that the Germans intended to deport the entire Jewish
population of the Netherlands to the east (that is, to occupied
Poland, where almost all of them were exterminated in purpose-
built camps), her father said that it would be an honour to give
his life for God's ancient people. Before they were betrayed by
Dutch neighbours and imprisoned, Corrie and her family saved
as many Jews as possible by hiding them. Thirty-five members
of this group of righteous Christians were arrested. Corrie was
kept in solitary confinement at Scheveningen and later at Vught
concentration camp, then sent to the appallingly cruel concentration camp for women at Ravensbruck, Germany, where her sister
died. Her father had already perished. Corrie ten Boom's letters
testify to her unshaken faith 'in Jesus Christ in the midst of the
deepest human evil'.

Corrie ten Boom, *A Prisoner Yet* (London, 1954); *Prison Letters* (London,
1975)

TERESA of Avila (St) (1515–82)

Spanish mystic, autobiographer, spiritual writer, and Doctor of the Church

Teresa was born in Avila, Spain. In about 1535, she became a nun in the Carmelite Convent of the Incarnation as Teresa de Jesús. She came to believe that the order's discipline ought to be reformed in accordance with her notions of primitive observance. In 1562, in spite of long periods of illness and much opposition from powerful enemies, including the Inquisition, she founded a new convent, and later sixteen others, in Spain. Together with St John of the Cross she was responsible for similar reforms among the friars. She was an extremely perceptive and responsible governor of and provider for her houses. She was also a great mystic, able to convey her extremely varied experiences in subtly composed literary works that are profound, strict, tender, amusing, realistic, psychologically acute, and sublimely ecstatic, as the occasion or circumstance demands. They include one of the world's great autobiographies and a multitude of letters. Like many original works they aroused much suspicion among the dull, authoritarian and small-minded.

The Letters of Saint Teresa of Avila, tr. and ed. E. Allison Peers (London, 1951); St Teresa of Avila, *The Way of Perfection*, tr. A Benedictine of Stanbrook, rev. B. Zimmerman OCD (London, 1961); 'The Interior Castle', in *The Complete Works of St Teresa of Jesus*, tr. and ed. E. Allison Peers (London, 1963); *The Life of St Teresa of Avila by Herself*, tr. D. Lewis, ed. D. Knowles (London, 1962); E. Sackville-West, *The Eagle and the Dove* (London, 1943); E. W. Trueman Dicken, *The Crucible of Love* (London, 1963); S. Clissold, *St Theresa of Avila* (London, 1978).

THÉRÈSE of Lisieux (St) (1873–97)

French nun, autobiographer, poet, dramatist and Doctor of the Church

Thérèse Martin was born into an intensely religious Norman family. She was the last of nine children, of whom five girls survived; all became nuns. Thérèse's mother died when she was just four years old. At fifteen Thérèse became a Carmelite nun in the convent at Lisieux and took the name 'of the Child Jesus', to which she later added 'and the Holy Face'. She was made novice-mistress of her convent but suffered from extreme ill-health. In spite of the obscurity of her short life, her 'little way' and her approach to the execution of everyday tasks and duties with care and humility were soon immensely influential among all sorts and conditions of people. She was asked to write her autobiography by her Mother Superior. She died of tuberculosis aged twenty-four. Her heavily edited *Journal of a Soul* subsequently became extremely popular and has had a universal influence.

Thérèse de l'Enfant-Jésus et de La Sainte Face, *Histoire d'une Âme* (Lisieux, 1898); *Oeuvres Complètes* (Paris, 2001); *Story of a Soul*, tr. J. Clarke (Washington, DC, 1975); *Poems of St Thérèse of the Child Jesus*, tr. Carmelites of Santa Clara (London, 1925); *Lettres de Sainte Thérèse de Lisieux de l'Enfant Jésus*, ed. A. Combes (Paris, 1948); *Collected Letters of Saint Thérèse of Lisieux*, tr. F. J. Sheed (London and New York, 1949); Ida Görres, *The Hidden Face: A Study of St Thérèse of Lisieux* (London, 1959); Felicity Leng, *Smiles of God: The Flowers of St Thérèse of Lisieux* (London, 2003).

UNDERHILL, Evelyn (1875–1941)

Anglican spiritual writer and theologian, director and counsellor

Evelyn Underhill was the daughter of a leading English barrister, and was educated at the largely C. of E. King's College, London. She was interested in religion from an early age. After flirtations with spiritualism and Roman Catholicism, which she resisted mainly because of her husband's antipathy to Rome, but also because of Pope Pius X's persecution of the Modernists, she became an intense student of mysticism. She was enthusiastically involved in high-church Anglicanism, as a full communicant from 1921, although her spiritual mentor remained the RC Baron von Hügel. Her *Mysticism* went into many editions and is still influential. She developed interests in ecumenism, social Christianity, and full Christian pacifism (an attitude which she maintained during World War II), and from 1924 was a popular conductor of retreats. She published many books and essays on mysticism and mystics, liturgy and aspects of Christian responsibility. The Episcopal Church of the USA commemorates her on 15 June.

Evelyn Underhill, *The Grey World* (London, 1904); *Mysticism* (London, 1911); *Concerning the Inner Life with the House of the Soul* (London, 1947); *Collected Papers of Evelyn Underhill*, ed. Lucy Menzies (London, 1946); *The Letters of Evelyn Underhill*, ed. Charles Williams (London, 1943); Margaret Cropper, *Life of Evelyn Underhill* (London, 1958); C. J. Armstrong, *Evelyn Underhill: An Introduction to Her Life and Writings* (London, 1975); *Evelyn Underhill on Prayer*, ed. Tony Castle (London, 1989).

WARD, Mary (1585–1645)

English founder, teacher and spiritual guide

Mary Ward was born in Yorkshire and baptized a Catholic. She became an 'out-sister' of the Poor Clares of St-Omer in 1606, and set up a daughter-house in Gravelines. After three years she left the convent, recruited five other women in England, went back to St-Omer, and founded what became the Institute of the Blessed Virgin Mary, the first unenclosed Catholic order for active rather than contemplative women, without enclosure or choir offices. Similar houses were established in Liège, Cologne, Rome, and other places. Ward's Institute was subject directly to the Pope, not to a bishop. The authorities sensed the dangers of such near-autonomy, suppressed the Institute in 1631, and confined Ward to the Convent of the Poor Clares in Munich. Eventually she was freed and went to Rome to obtain papal permission for her Institute to operate informally. In 1639 she returned to England and died near York. Her organization has led a chequered life but persists as three Institutes with three General Superiors.

Mary C. E. Chambers, *The Life of Mary Ward, 1585–1645*, ed. Henry James Coleridge, 2 vols (London, 1882–5); Mother M. Salome, *Mary Ward: A Foundress of the 17th Century* (London, 1901); Emmanuel Orchard IBVM, ed., *Till God Will: Mary Ward Through Her Writings* (London, 1985).

WEIL, Simone (1909–43)

French philosopher, social theorist and writer

Simone Weil was born into a secularized Jewish family in Paris. She studied philosophy and became a teacher. She developed an interest in sociology and left-wing politics, worked as a labourer at the Renault motor works for a year and then joined the International Brigade to fight for the Republicans in Spain. When teaching became a prohibited profession for Jews after the German occupation of France and the collaboration of the French authorities in the persecution and murder of people of Jewish ancestry, she worked on a farm in the unoccupied zone. In May 1942 she escaped to New York with her family, then worked for the Free French government in exile in London, where she followed the diet typical of wartime France. She died of tuberculosis in an English sanatorium. For many years Weil remained an agnostic but in later life developed a non-dogmatic, enquiring and near-mystical Christianity. She identified with the industrial labourer as the ideal type of suffering humanity in a world bent on dehumanization. She opposed all forms of domination and injustice. Her posthumously published works are tapestries of profound if sometimes enigmatic religious insights. The beauty of the world and the problems of time and humans' increased suffering because they know they are imprisoned in time yet are essentially driven to transcend it are among her main themes.

Simone Weil, *La Pesanteur et la Grâce* (Paris, 1947); *Gravity and Grace* (London, 1952); *L'Attente de Dieu* (Paris, 1950); *Lettre à un religieux* (Paris, 1951); *La Source grecque* (Paris, 1953); *L'Enracinement* (Paris, 1949); *La Condition ouvrière* (Paris, 1951); *Oppression et liberté* (Paris, 1955); *Écrits historiques et politiques* (Paris, 1960); S. Pétrement, *Simone Weil: A Life* (London, 1945); E. W. F. Tomlin, *Simone Weil* (London, 1954); G. A. White, *Simone Weil: An Interpretation* (London, 1981).

WHITE, Anna (late nineteenth century)

Shaker writer

Anna White was an elder of the North Family in the New Lebanon Shaker community at Mount Lebanon, New York. She wrote verse, and religious works on the meaning of Shakerism and the Shaker notion of the motherhood of God and the messianic role of the founder, Ann Lee, but her main contribution was as a historian of the Shaker communities and way of life.

Anna White and Leila S. Taylor, *Shakerism: Its Meaning and Message* (Columbus, OH, 1905); Anna White, *The Motherhood of God* (Mount Lebanon, New York, n.d.); Robert Edward Whitson, ed., *The Shakers: Two Centuries of Spiritual Reflection* (New York and Mahwah, NJ, 1984).

Biographies and Bibliographies

YONGE, Charlotte M. (1823–1901)

English novelist, editor and writer on religion

Charlotte lived all her life at Otterbourne near Winchester. She was a devoted member of the Church of England in the Tractarian, or non-Romanizing high-church, tradition as represented by John Keble, who became a local vicar and had an immense influence on Charlotte's spirituality. She was a skilful and prolific novelist, and *The Heir of Redclyffe* (1853) was a great popular success. This and other novels, though highly entertaining, were essentially didactic presentations of the duty v. inclination dilemmas of young Anglican women and their suitors and parents. She wrote lives of Hannah Moore and of the martyred Bishop Patteson of Melanesia, a far-sighted churchman who believed in devising a Christianity based on indigenous practice (she donated the proceeds of central works to the Solomon Islands missions). She also published children's books and historical fiction, translated a great deal, and edited a magazine for girls, *The Monthly Packet*. She never married.

Charlotte Yonge, *The Heir of Redclyffe* (London, 1853); *The Daisy Chain* (London, 1856); Christabel Coleridge, *Charlotte Mary Yonge: Her Life and Letters* (London, 1903); G. Battiscombe, *Charlotte Mary Yonge* (London, 1943); Robert Lee Woolff, *Gains and Losses: Novels of Faith and Doubt in Victorian England* (London and New York, 1977); B. Dennis, *Charlotte Yonge (1823–1901), Novelist of the Oxford Movement* (Lampeter, 1992).

Acknowledgements

The author and publisher thank John Griffiths for permission to use unpublished translations of verse and prose by Ann Griffiths © John Griffiths 2006.

Gratefully acknowledgement is also made for the kind permission of the following to reprint and/or adapt extracts from published works:

Continuum Publishing Company Ltd for:
A History of Christian Spirituality by Leclerq, Vandenbroucke and Bouyer © Burns & Oates Ltd 1968.
Broken Lights by Ida Friederike Görres © Burns & Oates Ltd 1964.
Smiles of God by Felicity Leng © Felicity Leng 2003.
Collected Letters of St Thérèse of Lisieux tr. F. J. Sheed © Sheed & Ward 1949.

Charles Crawford for *A Mirror for Simple Souls*, ed. & tr. C. Crawford © Charles Crawford 1981.

Desclée de Brouwer and the Estate of Raïssa Maritain for 'Douceur du Monde' from *Poèmes et Essais* by Raïssa Maritain © Desclée de Brouwer 1968.

John Cumming for *Letters from Saints to Sinners*, ed. John Cumming © John Cumming 1996.